FEBRUARY 6, 2012
MARJORIE AND NICK
FOR OLD FRIENDS WHO HAVE
SOUND VALUES.

ENJOY AND BE INSPIRED
I HAVE WANTED TO DO THIS
FOR A LONG TIME
JOHN

AMERICA ADRIFT

RIGHTING THE COURSE

AMERICA ADRIFT

RIGHTING THE COURSE

The Decline of America's Great Values

John W. Zimmerman Sr.

iUniverse, Inc.
Bloomington

America Adrift—Righting the Course
The Decline of America's Great Values

iUniverse books may be ordered through booksellers or by contacting:

iUniverse
1663 Liberty Drive
Bloomington, IN 47403
www.iuniverse.com
1-800-Authors (1-800-288-4677)

ISBN: 978-1-4620-5939-3 (sc)
ISBN: 978-1-4620-7102-9 (hc)
ISBN: 978-1-4620-7103-6 (ebk)

Library of Congress Control Number: 2011962178

Printed in the United States of America

iUniverse rev. date: 12/20/2011

Contents

Acknowledgment

I could not have completed this book without the dedicated help of my wife, Charlotte, who read, edited, and made creative and positive contributions to each succeeding version and worked with me as she typed those corrections and additions. Our son John devoted considerable time to getting the manuscript in a proper format with the many endnotes correctly noted. He, along with our other sons—Paul, Mark, and Jim—read the manuscript and made valuable suggestions to improve it. A big thanks to my granddaughter, Sarah Zimmerman, to my good friend Rex Kastner, and the family of Jerry Louvier (now deceased), who let me use examples from their lives.

I need to recognize my parents, Gladys and Wallace Zimmerman, who started me with sound and positive values. Again, I need to thank Charlotte, who continues to reinforce and strengthen those values and their application to my decision making, behavior, and relationships with others. I owe my now-deceased colleague, close friend, mentor, business partner, and boss, Ben Tregoe, so much for showing me the importance of values or beliefs as drivers of our business decisions and in our work with clients. Finally, I need to thank my best college friend, Jim Moore, for telling me about Jerry Louvier.

Ted Schroder, our good friend and pastor at the Amelia Plantation Chapel, Amelia Island, Florida, and Bill Gower, Amelia Island FL,founder and CEO of Matrix Inc. were kind enough to read the manuscript, provide valuable critique, and write a piece for the back cover. Thank you, Ted and Bill, for your support.

Introduction

I am passionate about the importance of sound and positive values to drive decision making, behavior, and relationships. Thus, it is tragic to see, with increasing frequency, the decline of those values that made America great and respected—honesty, trust, loyalty, commitment, moderation, hard work, self-fulfillment, health, and the like.

Stopping that decline and turning those values around is critical for the continued function of the family, the development of our children, and the sustainability of all the segments and institutions in our society—politics, government, education, religion, community, the workplace, business, and professions.

I believe the only hope for righting the course is for a majority of Americans who have sound values, love their country, and understand our ethics decline to share their values and lifestyles with those in need. If we cannot make that happen, I fear the promise for our grandchildren and all who follow will be lost and possibly our survival as a nation.

That is why I have written this book. Chapter 1 is dedicated to convincing you of the serious problems created across all segments of our society by this decline in values and their application. To demonstrate the full impact of this decline, I have included a number of research studies and commentaries that specifically show the disturbing results and trends in each segment of our society. Chapter

2 traces how personal values develop as one grows to adulthood. I used my own life as the example, as I knew it best. What values are, where they come from, and how they guide one's life are essential background components for chapters 3 and 4. Chapter 3 provides a rich source of ideas and examples to help improve your values and their application. Chapter 4 is the essence for action from this book. It describes how to take values and lifestyles to others in need. To help guide your thinking, many charitable organizations that are engaged in this critical effort are presented along with creative ideas and actions by individuals and groups.

Americans can accomplish anything they see as important to their community and country when they put their minds and efforts to it!

Chapter 1

What Happened to American Values

Our nation—once proud, prosperous, and leading the world—is in trouble. Many of the values which made America respected and envied, such as honesty, trust, accountability, commitment, self-determination, hard work, and moderation, are in decline. As a consequence, family stability, personal health and accountability, community responsibility, educational performance, sustainable government, business practices, and church involvement are often failing and unacceptable. It is imperative we turn this around.

There is significant effort by business and government; our educational, religious, and community structures; the many charitable social service organizations; and the millions of individual volunteer hours and dollars to right this course. This has lessened the slope of this decline *but* not turned the tide.

The only hope I see to assure our country's promise for those who follow is through the collective power of Americans who love their country, will help preserve its dream for the future, have sound and positive values, and have a reasonably effective, contributing, and loving life. To accomplish this, the seriousness of the problems created by this decline need understanding and acceptance. That is chapter 1. Then, it is necessary we know what values are, where they come from, and how they guide our lives. That is chapter 2. With that clear, we can explore our values and beliefs and make sure they are on the right path. That is chapter 3. Finally, we can take action—increase our willingness to share our values and positive life experiences with those individuals, families, communities, and societal organizations that are in need of help with values and results. That is chapter 4.

Marshaling the amount of human power this will take requires leadership. That must come from America's great leaders from all segments of society. Through the values of our business and professional leaders must come the motivation, opportunities and structure for their employees to get involved. From religious leaders must come the dedication of their great moral principles to this cause and a structuring within their congregations to make it happen. From educational leaders must come a clear understanding of best practices and the values behind them and then involve teachers, students, and parents to make that happen. From governmental leaders must come long-term policies and laws that will sustain our great values in programs, projects, and practices applied by all who work at federal, state, and local levels. From community and local service organization leaders must come better ways to organize and relate their activities and members so as to significantly increase the overall worth and structure of their communities.

That kind of leadership will build a power base to see that sound values guide the decisions that determine the long-term viability and future of all segments of our society. This book is written for those leaders and the "silent values majority" that will get the job done.

Values are the basic beliefs, principles, and concepts that guide and drive our decision making, behavior, and relationships with others. In a free and democratic society, the values held collectively by individuals and families shape those values that guide the nation and its government, business and civic organizations, religious structure, education system, community activities, and the like. Thus, it is the collective responsibility of our citizens to see that sound and positive values are reviewed and upheld, better applied, and thoughtfully reinterpreted over time as new changes prevail. A value like honesty is eternal and must be carefully and positively interpreted in a changing world. A value like equality, which has been misapplied in the past, must be applied equally to all citizens in regard to policies, practices, and the law. As new lifestyles about marriage and the family, the right to life, the right to organize, and the like emerge, they should be tested against their impact on sound ethics and the long-term consequences to our society. Throughout this book, the words *virtues, principles, beliefs, code of behavior,* and *ethical standards* are used interchangeably with *values*.

I might choose different words to express the following quote. You might also, and you may disagree with some of his conclusions. You may feel a prayer is no way to open this chapter. But his points, viewed from an overall perspective, support my thesis for this chapter and this book.

When Joe Wright, pastor of the Central Christian Church in Wichita, was asked to open the new session of the Kansas Senate with prayer, everyone expected the usual generalities, but this is an excerpt of what they heard:

We have lost our spiritual equilibrium and inverted our values.
We have exploited the poor and called it the lottery.
We have rewarded laziness and called it welfare.
We have killed our unborn and called it choice.
We have shot abortionists and called it justifiable.
We have neglected to discipline our children and called it building esteem.
We have abused power and called it political savvy.
We have coveted our neighbors' possessions and called it ambition.

3

We have polluted the air with profanity and pornography and called it freedom of expression.
We have ridiculed the time-honored values of our forefathers and called it enlightenment.[1]

To be fair, the application of some of our great, national basic beliefs has improved. We have done much to improve our value regarding equality. We have improved the position and quality of life for minorities and the role of women at work and in leadership. We are making good strides in applying values to protect and improve our long-term environment—the "greening" of America (and the world).

However, the great majority of the people I talk with feel quite strongly that many of the values or beliefs which made America the greatest free nation in the world are in significant decline or have been compromised—trust, honesty, loyalty, hard work, self-determination, pride, and the like. Not everyone I share ideas with feels that way, including some of my children. They are among the family-oriented, hardworking, and productive adults in the fifty-plus age bracket and in the prime of life. They feel basic values have always adapted to fit decisions and positions of the times. But many in that group also recognize that some of those value changes have produced outcomes that need improving in such areas as politics, education, and business, as well as community, family, and health care.

I am quite sure that many teens and younger adults, without the perspective of time and experience, feel that the current values that drive their decisions and behavior are just as they should be. I still remember as a teenager how important it was to fit in and behave like others in the group. That has always been and will continue to be in the future. I also know that, to some extent, each generation feels that the values guiding decision making and behavior today are not clear and "pure" as they were in "our days." The viewpoint of Coleman Langshaw in the following essay well supports this point:

It was the best of times, the worst of times

The sky is falling, the sky is falling . . . The world today is on the brink of destruction, moral decay at home and war overseas, the rich getting richer and the rest falling further behind. There are gangs fighting in the cities and the politicians are always lying. Our country is falling apart. Sound familiar? It should, it's a refrain that has been said forever.

In 1917, the 'War to End All Wars' was raging in Europe and the Bolsheviks were leading the way in turning everything upside down. Alcohol and drug abuse was rampant, immigrant gangs were prowling the streets of New York and other big cities, killing and stealing as they went. The Robber Barons like Carnegie, Rockefeller, Morgan, et al. were reaping vast fortunes on the backs of labor, and the new generation was challenging the status quo; women wanted to vote.

During the Roaring Twenties, it was 'party time' for the rich, booze flowed and flappers were dancing. Oh, the outrage that permeated from the establishment. The young were going wild, showing off their bare arms and calves, what was happening to our values?

Then there was the Great Depression, and things were truly falling apart, and the blame fell on the decadence of the past. In reality, part of that was probably true. People drunk with money and selfishness did suddenly wake up to the horror of bankruptcy and the world crumbling down. But there were many reasons, and it took a principle of having nothing to fear but fear itself to make our nation realize that eventually this too will pass.

And then there was another World War, reaching around the globe and once again the dark clouds of concern that our world was perhaps coming to an end returned. Horrific genocide and the atomic bombs understandably spoke of the unraveling of decency and sanity. What happened to the simpler and better times of yesteryear? But, of course, those were not simpler and better times, they were just different from earlier times; people survived and continued on.

The Cold War, the Korean 'Conflict,' Vietnam, all too brought out the sense that our country and also the world was falling apart. Even in the seemingly mild and apple pie 1950s the kids were going wild. 'Elvis the Pelvis' was disgusting the older and conservative generation, James Dean humanized the rebels without a cause, Hollywood was a strange dreamland of unreality, everybody in school was learning to 'duck and cover' under their schoolroom desks and racism was alive and well on buses and schools and in everyday life in the 'land of freedom and equality.'

The 1960s, well, those numbers sum it all up for most people. Protests, riots, war overseas, political corruption, the kids and the moral decay, love-ins, rock 'n' roll. Our country was falling apart. Once again, the familiar refrain: What happened to the simpler and better times of yesteryear? And again, those were not simpler and better times, they were just different than earlier times; people survived and continued on.

The '70's had Watergate and the first president to resign from office in disgrace, the first energy crisis, a hostage crisis in Iran and we started hearing the frequent term 'terrorists.' And the economy was tanking (once again). Our country was falling apart, or at least it seemed that way.

In the '80's and '90's money became the long hair of those decades, and scandals raged, greed was rampant and a new 'Me Generation' was booming. Drugs and gangs were as deadly as ever. Moral decay and the new generation seemed to go hand-in-hand, or so it seemed at the time.

And, as always, people harkened back to the better times, whenever that supposedly was; Time and memories, re-writing history, softening the past to create a stark comparison to the current events.

So here we are today, in the worst of times, so people think. We are living in a time when terrorism is shaking us to the core. We are living in a time when the new generation supposedly has no values or morals; we are telling ourselves that things were better in the past.

Yes, it is true that we are living in dangerous and tumultuous times. But we have always lived in such times. In 1860, our nation was in a Civil War—an unfathomably, terrible time, but we survived. The course of human events is like that, but they are never time-specific.

We must not, and cannot, look at our present time and throw up our arms and yell that the sky is falling. We should not forget the lessons of the past, both terrible and great, and simply explain away life today as crumbling from moral decay and blame the next generation as the symbol of our troubles.

The future of our country and the world is serious and uncertain, but if we don't succumb to the latest version of the age-old refrain, and embrace the opportunities that lie ahead, we will thrive as we always have. We really do have nothing to fear but fear itself.[2]

I agree with the author's "great-terrible-we-survived" repetition over time. However, I believe there are major changes going on across the world now that, taken together, affect the future of America far more than the magnitude of events of the past. There are nations and significantly increasing numbers of radical and self-sacrificing terrorists whose ultimate goal is to bring America and the free world down and force their beliefs and lifestyles on us. There are many groups and nations who are against terrorist motives and actions but do little about them. We live in a global world economy with emerging nations that can be more productive, aggressive, and powerful than America at its best. Our once-proud status as the world's best provider of quality industrial products and foods and the great protector of freedom continues to decline. America is now a significant importer of goods. That means the wealth we once created and that made us a big exporter of goods is now moving elsewhere. Some argue that net importer nations over time may go bankrupt. Too much of our industrial base—which always was our bulwark and strength—has moved out of America. There is a little good news in that, recently, some of it may be coming back. Too many governments and citizens live beyond their means, and the world owns our resulting debt. They could foreclose at some point, and they would own us. Our federal debt is beyond comprehension, and our government appears unable to deal with it, causing doubt for our future.

We are the government! Our values have changed such that a majority elects, and reelects, candidates who do short-term things and fail to deal with major issues. Our immediate comfort and benefit seems paramount. Sacrifice for the longer term is becoming beyond our ability to fathom, and so, our government reflects our short-term values and outlook—it doesn't set them! So, at the federal level, we ignore potential huge Social Security, Medicare, and Medicaid shortfalls and ignore the long-term consequences of bailout debt, health care costs, and unprecedented deficit spending. Those are left for some future leaders to handle. At the state level, we build more prisons and put little into prevention. At the local level, we provide incentives to developers with too little thought as to who will pay for services then required. At all levels, unrealistic and underfunded long-term benefits are bargained away to union leaders to avoid dispute and disruption without much thought about how they will be paid for and who will pay for them in the future. As the old cliché says, "What goes around comes around."

The disparity in America between the "haves" and the "have nots" continues to grow. That means the middle class, which was a bright strength, is shrinking. Many nations, both industrial and developing, no longer like or respect America. The developing world is overtaking our innovative leadership and surpassing our rank in many critical skills like education, which is required for future growth and prosperity. Currently, America and a lot of the rest of the world is faced with major financial, housing, credit, economic, and federal debt problems with scope and characteristics from which even experts do not know how long it may take to recover—if ever.

The complexity of these issues and how to resolve them presents major challenges. I believe the best way to address them—and the lessons from Greece and Rome—is to turn our values in a more positive direction and broaden their application. Then, decisions, behavior, and relationships must be driven by those renewed, positive, and tested principles.

This is a very ambitious goal and will be difficult to accomplish. I am neither a learned professor researching and teaching ethics nor have I been a compliance or ethics officer in a major corporation overseeing the development and application of its beliefs. I have, however, spent my career helping develop a successful, worldwide consulting firm that had sound basic beliefs, and used them to guide our decisions. We helped our clients shape and apply their code of ethics to strategic and operational decision making. I married a wonderful woman with sound and uplifting virtues, and together, we raised four sons with those virtues as a basic cornerstone for their lives. Throughout my life, I have been involved with volunteer organizations and have helped them apply their ethical standards to their efforts. I have a tremendous passion for the importance of sound values and their unique ability to influence the decisions and behavior of individuals, families, communities, and our nation, which will lead to the brighter future we all desire.

I am driven to write this small book because my strong belief is that every noble American should do more to take on this challenge personally in what they do and how they live. And, it is up to America's leaders in every walk of life to mobilize and lead that charge. When that happens, America's promise will be assured, and your grandchildren and their children will enjoy the benefits and appreciate your efforts.

In later chapters, I will suggest practical guidelines and examples of how to begin to accomplish these value-driven societal-improvement goals. But before we get to the prescription, we need to understand the scope and urgency of the problem. Taken one by one, the following research studies and statistics about negative outcomes and the values and beliefs leading to them could be explained away by proclaiming that

- good things also happen around each situation;
- the data was not properly collected or evaluated;
- the author is biased;
- there have always been such situations;
- statistics can be used to prove or disprove anything; and
- it is next to impossible to get truly accurate data.

Nevertheless, these trends and outcomes taken as a whole have shown me—and I hope will convince you—that our great American values and beliefs are being consistently eroded. And if we let these trends continue, the bright future of our nation will be darkened.

While I stand on the previous paragraph, and before getting into that story, let me be very clear on my beliefs about the positive side. American business, from giant Exxon Mobil and Walmart down to the local jewelry and shoe store, is the engine that drives our economy. It creates good-paying jobs, causes growth of the middle class, develops innovative new products and services, provides returns for its investors, supports its communities, and pays taxes.

The model American family of a father, mother, children, and often nearby relatives is the backbone for sound values, decisions, and behavior for its members, their community, and society in general. While the family is still the driving force, it is sad to see it coming apart along with the quality of life it provided. For the first time in history, families living in marriage have fallen below 50 percent. We need to bring it back!

While there are many excellent public and private schools, colleges, and universities in America, we are falling behind the world in the quality of our graduates, our rates of graduation, and preparation of our graduates for work and life. Our great beliefs in self-determination, accountability, hard work, reward for performance, honesty, and parental responsibility seem to increasingly bypass what goes on in the educational system. We need to get to root causes and fix them. The fix will come from studying what excellent schools are doing differently and spread that application across the system.

There are many dedicated and ethical elected politicians and appointed officials and staff at all levels of government. But there are too many who are driven by their own egos to stay in office, promise a lot, and deliver much less—most of it short term. It is time that we, as voters, tested and elected more of the first kind and got rid of the second.

Our principles and beliefs are not the only factors that lead to the serious national issues and outcomes which follow. But they are a critical key. They drive the decisions we make, the behaviors we exhibit, and our relationships with others. The collective ethical standards of our society as a whole have significantly influenced where we stand on these issues. Depending on what we do with that stance in the future will determine whether those outcomes worsen or are turned in more positive directions. The future of America and what that means for our grandchildren is dependent on righting that values direction.

For each of those issues and outcomes, a wealth of data is presented as to the history, current status, and future trends. My goal was not to overwhelm you but rather to get you to feel and internalize the scope, depth, and seriousness of those trends taken in total. Then, you can judge their potential impact on our culture, lifestyle, and the future of the American dream and survival if left unchecked. Then, the fix is up to us!

The Values Issues

There is variation in some of the following statistics depending on scope and accuracy of data and the methodology applied. I have used more than one source when possible.

Trust

Wikipedia defines trust as "a prediction of reliance on an action based upon what a party knows about another party." *Free Merriam-Webster Dictionary* defines trust this way: "assured reliance on the character, ability, strength, or truth in someone . . . one in which confidence is placed." *American Heritage Dictionary of the English Language* says: "reliance on the integrity, strength, ability, surety, etc., of a person or thing; confidence." I like "reliance" as one key to trust. Reliance and trust can only develop through multiple actual or verifiable experiences with an individual, group, institution, or organization. For me, trust is about whom I would want holding the other end of the rope if I were dangling off a cliff!

The administration and the president face widening voter pessimism about trust, says a new *Wall Street Journal* poll taken August 27-31, 2011:

> 44% of Americans approve of the job Mr. Obama is doing with more than 51% disapproving for the first time since his inauguration. Some 73% say the country is headed in the wrong direction. More than 70% of the people surveyed say the economy hasn't as yet bottomed out. [3]

And Congress—with its low ratings—still takes care of itself. A 2010 Gallup poll reported:

> Only 13 percent of Americans say they approve of the job Congress is doing, which beats the old low of 14 percent from July, 2008 when gas prices reached record high on top of a bad economy.

And a Pew Survey in December of 2010 reported that:

> 72 percent of Americans are dissatisfied with national conditions. 67 percent say the country is losing ground on the budget deficit. 89 percent rate national economic conditions as fair or poor. 70 percent . . . said the federal budget deficit is a major problem and must be dealt with now. [4]

As partisan and divided as Congress is, one wonders if these serious conditions will be dealt with or put off again for future leaders. And with all that turmoil, they gave themselves a raise in 2008 and another one in 2009.

"With businesses all over the country cutting jobs, Congress saw fit to let an automatic 2.8 percent increase kick in. That's about $4,700 per member. A pay raise for what? A lack of regulation and lax rules by Congress are big factors in both the housing and the

Wall Street crises that have ensnared the country. In addition, this Congress has been ethically challenged, plagued with corruption allegations, convictions, and sex scandals." Congress now earns $174,000 per year. Legislation that would have prevented the raise died in committee. [5]

As far as Congress is concerned, it is hard for me to understand how one's conscience could stand accepting pay raises given such a lack of performance and disapproval. Those elected to our federal government need a higher standard around integrity, trust, responsibility, and the long versus the short term.

There is no doubt that trust and the reputation of big business has diminished given the financial and housing shenanigans and the 2008 recession along with the continued big executive bonus payouts—not always tied to performance. This poll by the Marist Institute for Public Opinion reports the following:

A survey of 2071 Americans and 110 high-level business leaders shows that "a whopping 94 percent of Americans and 93 percent of executives said corporate executives make decisions based on advancing their own careers; 69 percent of Americans responding said commitment to public good rarely or never influenced their decisions, while 68 percent of upper executives agreed." When asked to rate honesty and ethical conduct on a scale of good-fair-poor respondents in another poll said: of politicians—10% good, 56% poor; of Wall Street executives—10% good, 61% poor; Corporate executives—14% good, 49% poor; of top executives in the financial and investment industry—13% good, 59% poor. [6]

While those in the corporate world of finance, banking, real estate, and Wall Street—who helped cause these lousy results—need to get out or take action to correct them, it is a shame to tar and feather all those American companies that operate on a sound and positive ethical code of conduct.

In 2008, we were faced with a housing and financial disaster that led to an economic recession. This is a classic example of what can happen to good intentions when sound values get lost in the actions to implement them. It began with Congress acting on its positive desire to deregulate the banking industry and its irresponsibility to then establish surveillance and controls to protect the consumer and the banking industry from itself. Next, Congress acted on its good intention to provide more home ownership for lower-income families. They had Fannie Mae and Freddie Mac execute that desire through the banking/lending industry with no thought as to the consequences that could develop. So the big banks created clever ways to attract those new home buyers with their profit motive in mind and not the circumstances of their customers. And too many of those new home buyers thought only of the potential financial gain in what they were doing and not the risks they were taking. Then, the greed of Wall Street bundled those good and not-so-good subprime mortgages into instruments to sell to investors. Wall Street—and those investors—thought too much about their gain and too little about what could happen if things turned down. And in the midst of all this mess, many who helped to cause the problems took home nice fat bonuses as if their efforts had been a rousing success.

Now that all these thousands of foreclosures have occurred and are being processed, another scandal emerges. These guys can't seem to get their ethics right even when trying to fix the problems they created. The Associated Press reports the following:

"In an effort to rush through thousands of home foreclosures since 2007, financial institutions and their mortgage servicing departments hired hair stylists, Walmart floor workers, and people who had worked on assembly lines, and installed them in 'foreclosure expert' jobs with no formal training, a Florida lawyer says. In depositions released Tuesday (October 12, 2010) many of those workers testified they barely knew what a mortgage was. Peter Tickin, a Deerfield Beach lawyer, who is defending 3000 homeowners, gathered 150 depositions from bank employees who say they signed foreclosure affidavits without reviewing the documents or ever laying eyes on them—earning them the name 'robo-signers.' A former senior partner in Stern's law firm (foreclosure king David Stern) described a boiler room atmosphere in which employees were pressured to forge signatures, backdate documents, swap social security numbers, inflate billings, and pass around notary stamps as if they were salt." This is all leading to legal challenge. [7]

This is likely to prolong the housing depression at least another few years. Worst of all is the financial and emotional suffering by all those who were defrauded.

In many ways, all of the above was caused by a failure to apply sound virtues to the application of good intentions so as to obtain realistic short—and long-term gains with minimum adverse consequences.

With all these devastating results from shenanigans, greed, and lack of control being well publicized, the con game goes on:

"Say you commit a really serious crime. It's likely your bond will be set at a price too steep to afford. You'll sit in jail until your case is heard." But you are not Bernie Madoff who swindled billions from his investors and ruined families and triggered suicides. "Not the man who apparently violated the order that allowed him to live in 'house arrest' in his luxury Manhattan home even after he 'gifted' over $1 million in jewels to close friends." [8]

The sound and lasting ethical standards that should have guided decisions by Congress, the president, banks and other lenders, Wall Street, and prospective home buyers often turned instead to short-term opportunism, the failure to assess long-term risks, greed, and downright dishonesty. What a tragic shame that taking eyes off sound ethics led to good ideas going down the drain. As the song goes, "When Will We Ever Learn," or, as Oliver Goldsmith says in

The Deserted Village, "Ill fares the land, to hastening ills a prey / where wealth accumulates, and men decay . . ."

It would seem few sound and positive values, such as trust and honesty, were applied by those responsible for these situations, and I hope they all will be held accountable and punished accordingly.

And now, Congress has passed a huge and complex health care bill. It was conceived in a partisan way by one party with little input by the other party. That led to a bitter debate and ultimately to providing favors to obtain the necessary votes just to pass it. While it brings many more into our health care system, there is little assurance that it will improve overall quality of health care or control costs. It is very likely that the premiums we pay for health insurance will increase. Some knowledgeable experts believe the longer-range costs in terms of federal debt will be huge. The sad part is that those who really will have to cope with this huge burden are our children and grandchildren.

Waste and fraud in the federal government is constantly reported, but it seems little is done to remove it:

> A 2005 report by the National Academy of Engineering and the Institute of Medicine found that 30 cents to 40 cents of every dollar spent on health care is wasted. [9]

According to an analysis by Brian Reidl of the Heritage Foundation:

> The excuse one hears most often is: that there is no place legislators can cut spending. Really? Government auditors spent the last five years examining all federal programs and found that 22 percent of them—costing taxpayers $123 billion per year—fail to show any positive impact on the populations they serve. [10]

According to SAS:

> Government agencies face enormous challenges in attempting to prevent improper payments caused by fraud, waste and abuse. The US Office of Management and Budget estimated that the government lost more than $125 billion in improper payments in fiscal year 2010 alone—a conservative estimate at best. And it's the taxpayer who ends up footing the bill. [11]

No wonder we don't trust Congressional politicians. And, that same lack of trust often carries over to state and local governments.

As far as lack of trust and accountability at colleges and universities, here is an example of what your students are being exposed to. The *New York Times* reports the following:

"The bank (Bank of America) has an $8.4 million seven-year contract with Michigan State giving it access to students' names and addresses and use of the university's logo. The more students who take the bank's credit cards, the more money the university gets. Under certain circumstances Michigan State even stands to receive more money if students carry a balance on these cards." Students learn about and get involved with credit, often for the first time, leading to the chance of spending more than their means: one study shows seniors with $2,630 average credit card debt. [12]

These practices take place at major state and public universities which are supported by your students' tuition and your taxes.

When trust begins to break down in our institutions of higher learning, that is a value decline with scary consequences. They are preparing our leaders of the future.

Honesty or Integrity

Free Merriam-Webster Dictionary defines honesty as "not lying, cheating, or stealing; fairness and straightforwardness of conduct." Breakdowns in this value often start with very small indiscretions and self-forgiving rationalizations like the following examples:

- It is not my fault the clerk gave me too much change and didn't charge properly for this.
- My friends do it, so why shouldn't I?
- It's just this one time.
- I'll bury this personal item in my expense account.
- So I kick the golf ball from behind the tree—that doesn't affect anyone else.

But when these fairly minor infractions expand to larger ones and end up becoming a way of life, this ethical decline impacts our societal health and future.

Earmarks have become a "way-to-beat-the-budget" lifestyle in the federal government. Earmarks are unfunded items or projects which sponsors try to get added to the budget by attaching them to upcoming bills. In the mammoth defense budget, they are put together by the military, the defense contractors, and members of Congress. Here is an example of how this works, taken from a *Business Week* investigation:

In 2004, after the navy had submitted its official budget, Admiral Vernon C. Clark signed off on another list of projects that had not been funded. This list began circulating among defense industry lobbyists. This list of 61 items included a request for a "C-37"—the equivalent of a Gulfstream G550 used by globe-trotting business CEOs and executives. Defense industry lobbyists began working Congress explaining that the Navy would add the plane to its Pacific fleet where officers had to travel long distances. The lobbying worked and the defense bill that year included a $53 million earmark to

19

fund the plane. Saxby Chambliss (a Georgia Republican, where Gulfstream as part of General Dynamics would produce the plane) took credit saying the earmark made sense for the navy since the G550 fit the service requirements for a long-range jet. The new plane never made it to the Pacific fleet as was the goal. It is housed at Andrews Air Force Base, near Washington DC, and designated for the use of . . . the Navy Secretary and the Chief of Naval Operations—the same office that had requested the earmark for the Pacific in the first place. A study suggested that companies make $28 in earmark revenue for every dollar they spent lobbying.

The sad history of earmarks features a long list of abuses: earmarks used by congressional leaders to buy votes on other legislation, earmarks sent to political donors, and earmarks used in outright bribery. Such issues continue to arise. While earmarks are down, many lobbyists predict earmark totals will bounce back once the spotlight fades. [13]

President Obama said in his campaign that he would be interested in legislation to suppress earmarks. Such legislation is being proposed by a group led by Senator John McCain. President Obama has now implied he will not support it because Representative Pelosi and Senator Reid oppose it.

Like defense, Medicare is another huge federal program—43.5 million people enrolled with an annual budget of $408 billion—that has inadequate controls to prevent resulting fraud which is running rampant:

> Federal agencies are trying to clamp down on fraud rackets that are thought to bill Medicare more than $620 million in 2006 in Florida alone. Phony billings for intravenous drugs, especially AIDS medicine and chemotherapy, is a hot area for fraud. Phony clinics now pay some retirees $100 or $150 a month to pretend they're patients and not to complain when fake charges show up on their records. At

least 170 companies have been suspended from payment: 270 more under investigation or automatically flagged for review. [14]

If that much cheating in Medicare is going on in Florida in one year, think what that is costing us taxpayers across the United States.

Cheating by MBA students almost seems the way to get ahead. A study of 5,331 graduate students at thirty-two schools in Canada and the United States, co-authored by Linda Trevino a professor at Penn State's Smeal College of Business, reports:

> . . . 56% of business grad students admitted to cheating in the past academic year. That's more than the 47% of nonbusiness grad students making the same admission. [15]

It starts in high school—probably earlier. Rutgers's Dr. Donald McCabe's national survey of 25,000 high school students from 2002 to 2008 showed 90% had cheated in various ways:

> The biggest deterrent is not the values that students are exposed to at home, but peer norms at school. Students are under pressure to achieve high grade-point averages, which helps them rationalize their behavior. And the schools themselves are complicit, because they reward high grades more than the process of learning—while too often turning a blind eye to the cheating. [16]

Cheating has become part of the acceptable status quo. Will these students continue with that value set as they grow to lead the future decisions and societal behavior of our nation?

Not only students but some high school administrators and teachers are not above reproach as far as integrity and trust:

"Former Atlanta schools Superintendent Beverly Hall knew about cheating allegations on standardized tests but either ignored them or tried to hide them, according to a state investigation made public Tuesday (July 5, 2011). The yearlong investigation shows educators at nearly four dozen Atlanta elementary and middle schools cheated on standard tests by helping students or changing the answers once exams were handed in. The investigators also found a 'culture of fear, intimidation, and retaliation' in the school district over the cheating allegations, which led to educators lying about the cheating or destroying documents to cover it up, according to the report. 'Dr. Hall and her administration emphasized test results and public praise to the exclusion of integrity and ethics.'" The results are being sent to prosecutors, and these cases could lead to criminal charges. [17]

When public schools' administrators and teachers have ethical standards that would allow that behavior, there are very serious consequences to their lives and the development of their students.

Unfortunately, when a values breakdown results in major trouble—like Enron—too often the values pendulum swings too far in correction. Regulations go too far. Generally Accepted Accounting Principles (GAAP) required financial institutions to value their assets not on what long-term history suggested but rather on current market value. It was called "mark to market." That caused havoc given the severe decline in housing values. Homes with historic value but still in mortgage became valued at the current severe downturn price. This significantly dropped banks' capital value on their books and caused them to seek more capital. But because of the current home values, there were no providers. Many have said that the mark-to-market standard is a primary cause of the current recession. This is particularly troublesome when all business gets painted with the Enron brush. Most have sound basic beliefs, and are not at all run like Enron.

But ethical problems do affect the world of business:

Most of us (69%) think taking home stuff from the office is wrong, according to a recent survey of more than 2100 employed adults. But almost 20% of us admit to doing it. The Office Theft Poll conducted in May (2007) by Harris Interactive for recruiter Spherion, also found that filching supplies—mostly pens, pencils, rulers, file folders, and Post-It notes—is more common among workers making at least $75,000 a year (23%) than it is among those making $15,000 to $34,999 (11%) and the No. 1 explanation from those who said they sneak out supplies? "I needed them." [18]

A good friend of mine told me a similar story. One of his responsibilities was the office supply cabinets for a very large manufacturing facility. He said, "When school was starting in the fall, we were like Walmart. The number of pens, notebooks, and paper withdrawn would go up dramatically."

I recall reviewing expense reports of those Associates who reported to me during my consulting career. Most followed our general expense guidelines, but others padded their reports with expenses far beyond what I considered reasonable. As I disallowed some of them, I always explained that they were professionals with an ethical, conservative firm that shared profits with them and that their compensation was based on performance and should not be aided by expense reports. My boss and I always followed this rule on our expense reports: when in doubt, leave it out.

When it comes to values, I have always believed in the "whole man" concept: if you violate integrity in one way or place, chances are you will violate it in other aspects of your life. There may be some who could, but I do not believe that most of us could cheat or lie at work and be true blue in the rest of our lives.

A lot of ethical/honesty concerns can be raised between a CEO and top executives and the company shareholders and employees in the matter of stock options:

In 1992 the SEC required that companies put in their proxy statements the dates stock options were given to top executives. With this data available, David Yermack, a New York University finance professor, looked at stock prices prior to and after options grants and found this consistent outcome. Based on 7,785 options grants to CEOs of 1970 companies between 1996 and 2005, stock prices went down about 1.5 percent over 30 days prior to the options grants and increased about 4 percent 30 days after the grants. Yermack figured that this was not just luck, and theorized that companies were timing their grants to precede good-news announcements and follow negative ones. Accounting professors David Aboody of UCLA and Ron Kasnik of Stanford followed up with an examination of companies that made options grants on more or less the same day every year, and found a similar pattern. Their theory: companies will publish the release of bad and good results to lower prices before grants and raise them afterwards.

That is dishonesty at top levels—even more serious:

Erik Lie of the University of Iowa noted that many options grants were timed to exploit market-wide price movements that no CEO could predict. At least some of the official grant dates must have been set retroactively, Lie suggested in a paper. Messing with options grant dates after the fact and lying about it in financial reports is illegal so Lie sent a copy of his findings to the SEC which began investigating. By the end of 2007, this scandal thus far has led to criminal charges at two companies and more than 40 senior executives losing their jobs. [19]

The total amount of money paid off in unethical, sometimes criminal, and nonperformance-based options and other incentives is money that could have been used to improve product quality or lower costs, increase employee pay, or provide shareholders with increased dividends.

Regardless of what the media says, before drawing a conclusion that doing away with incentives like options will fix the problem, consider this—and I am not forgiving the situation above. Financial incentives that are ethical and legal when given for long-term growth, job creation, product and market innovation, community involvement, and investor reward are powerful motivators. It is when these kinds of incentives are given for short-term gains with major long-term consequences or inadequate performance that does not meet goals or is not legal that ethics are of concern.

Consider this possibility. Congress becomes paid a very minimum base salary with incentives based on performance. Fixing Social Security earns an initial 10 percent bonus with 5 percent added each of the following two years if it is working. Creating a health care system that focuses on prevention, provides availability for all Americans, is cost-result effective, and utilizes private industry is worth a 15 percent initial bonus with 5 percent added each of the following two years if it is working. Doing away with earmarks earns 3 percent. Finding and eliminating waste earns 5 percent. And so on. Voters have solid information on which to judge their representatives, our long term is protected, and trust could be regained. Think of school superintendents and principals, university chancellors, and more business executives on this kind of program.

When it comes to dishonesty and fraud, nonprofit organizations have their share. An Ethics Resource Center nationwide survey shows the following:

The rapid growth of US nonprofits—revenues in the sector went from $678 billion in 1994 to $1.4 trillion in 2004—has brought with it a decline in ethical standards. Indeed, observations of fraud including doctored financial records and lying to stakeholders are now about as prevalent in nonprofits (with 55% of respondents saying they've seen examples) as they are for-profit (56%) and public (57%) sectors. "More nonprofits are larger in size, and with that you would expect to see organizations establishing ethics and compliance systems," says Patricia Harned, the Center's president, "but we're not seeing that." 58 charity fraud cases from the Certified Fraud Examiners Association's database . . . produce estimates that charities may lose as much as $40 billion per year to fraud. [20]

That is hard-earned money you and I donated!

Self-Improvement/Self-Determination

Let's start with high school dropout/graduation rates. The Alliance for Excellent Education in Washington DC reports the following:

- Every school day, nearly 7,000 high school students in the United States become dropouts.
- Only 70 percent of all entering freshmen, and slightly more than half the students of color, finish American high schools with a regular diploma.
- Only 30 percent of students entering high school read at grade level.
- Among developed nations, the United States ranks seventeenth in its high school graduation rate.

High school dropouts often can't find well-paying jobs, are less healthy, die younger, become parents when very young quite often, are more likely to become involved with the criminal justice system, and will probably need social welfare assistance. [21]

The military also has their problems with public education, according to the Education Trust:

A new study of 350,000 high school graduates ages 17-20 shows that "nearly one-fourth of the students who try to join the US Army fail its entrance exam, painting a grim picture of an education system that produces graduates who can't answer basic math, science and reading questions." This is a sample question: "Dana receives $30 for her birthday and $15 for cleaning the garage. If she spends $16 on a CD, how much money does she have left? A. $29; B. $27; C. $24; D $12." [22]

Michael E. Porter, a leading authority on competitive strategy and world competitiveness at the Harvard Business School, has this discouraging assessment of American public education. This is part of an article detailing several major strategic areas where America is in trouble:

All Americans realize that the public education system is in trouble, but not as many may know that those retiring today are better educated than those entering the workforce. "Without world-class education and skills, Americans must compete with workers in other countries for jobs that could be moved anywhere. Unless we significantly improve the performance of our public schools, there is no scenario in which many Americans will escape continued pressure on their standard of living. And legal and illegal immigration of low-skilled workers cannot help but make the problem worse for less-skilled Americans."

The issue is not money—we spend a considerable amount on public education. The real issue is how our education system is configured. "The states, for example, need to consolidate some of the 14,000 local school districts whose existence almost guarantees inefficiency and inequality of education across communities." Rather government leaders debate minor changes. [23]

While better methods for collecting and assessing data are needed, from all the surveys I reviewed, a good norm for national high school graduation is 70 percent, with minorities at 50 percent. That is not good enough!

A recent example of the power of those in control who don't want the boat rocked to challenge the status quo occurred in Washington DC:

Mayor Adrian Fenty knew the public school system needed drastic review and change. He appointed Michele Rhee as schools chancellor. Her approach to the "tough love" required to put the student's interests first included tying teacher evaluations to student test scores, removing low-performing educators, closing failing schools, adding merit pay to teachers' contracts, and giving vouchers to parents to provide more selections. During her 3 1/2 years students test scores improved as she worked to put them first. But she earned the wrath of the teachers' union. "The *Washington Post* reports that Ms. Rhee's resignation 'Won immediate support from the Washington Teachers' Union,' as strong signals that her departure is a victory for the adults who run public education, not the kids in failing schools." They spent $1,000,000 in support of Mr. Gray who defeated current Mayor Fenty in the primary and will be the next Mayor. [24]

While I would not support this position by the union, their rationale is obvious. That makes it more difficult to understand how that position was positively conveyed to the voters who cast the ballots and are the parents of the children in a failed public school system.

College graduation rates are equally disturbing. An article by Mark Schneider in the *Journal of the American Enterprise Institute* reports:

Statistics on college graduation rates are not too reliable but these are the only ones we have. For example some schools graduate hardly anyone and others almost everyone. Data from these National Center for Education Statistics reports that for the US four-year colleges graduation rates are 57.2% and for two year colleges 30.5%. [25]

David Leonhardt reports in the *New York Times* from a new book entitled *Crossing the Finish Line*:

The causes for these disturbing graduation rates are many. The biggest problem is the focus on enrollment rather than completion and the colleges are not held accountable for their failures.

Inadequate high school education is also a problem. Another issue is that high-achieving low-income students do not attend the best college they could: like the University of Michigan (graduation rate 88%). Rather they go to Eastern Michigan with a 39% graduation rate. So, large numbers do not graduate. And lastly, many students are not motivated to graduate in four years and graduation delayed often means no graduation. [26]

Much research must be done to determine why rates at universities with similar characteristics vary so much:

> For instance, the main campuses at Penn State and the University of Minnesota have comparable price tags, student SAT scores, and percentage of students from poor backgrounds. Yet, Penn State graduates more than 80% of its students and Minnesota barely half. [27]

Beliefs concerning accountability, commitment, hard work, and pride of accomplishment for all those who influence our high school and college educational systems need significant improvement. That would include administrators, teachers, boards, parents, students, and politicians. It also includes voters who ultimately can put those in power who really understand and care about educational issues and will address them.

In my opinion, these very disturbing results will not turn in more positive directions until we undertake nationwide research to identify excellent educational facilities, what factors make them so, and how to reproduce those factors across the United States. Research must include answers to the following questions:

- Is it the quality of high school education?
- Are too many young people going to four-year colleges and universities who probably should not be?
- Should more students attend community colleges, trade schools, or apprentice programs?

- Is it the students themselves?
- Is it the universities' fault for putting too many resources into getting students and not enough into how to keep them?
- Are schools allocating too high a percentage of their funds to administration and overhead and not enough directly to student education?

We need to find out!

It is obvious that education pays off and lack of education does not. According to the Bureau of Labor Statistics, 100 percent of new jobs by skill level breaks down as follows:

- Competent (some post-secondary education) 38%:
- Advanced (bachelor's degree or higher) 26%;
- Basic (high school graduate) 24%;
- Minimal (high school dropout) 12%. [28]

A 2010 population survey of people over twenty-five and working full time by the Bureau of Labor Statistics shows education, unemployment, and earnings:

Unemployment	Education	Median Weekly Earnings
1.9%	Doctoral degree	$1,550
2.4%	Professional degree	$1,610
4.0%	Master's degree	$1,272
5.4%	Bachelor's degree	$1,038
7.0%	Associate's degree	$ 767
9.2%	Some college	$ 712
10.3%	High school graduate	$ 526
14.9%	Non-high school graduate	$ 444

Physical, Mental, and Moral Health

The Centers for Disease Control and Prevention and the Guttmacher Institute report the following on abortion:

While the trend is downward since 1997, from the passage of Roe-Wade in 1973, there have been 53,300,000 abortions through 2010. These are actual figures for 1973 through 2008 and estimates for 2009 and 2010. [30]

Regardless of legality or one's personal position, the creation of that many potential babies and then their abortion suggests a value set that could stand more careful thought.

The ethics leading to decisions about drinking, drugs, smoking, and obesity are in much disarray. The National Institute on Alcohol Abuse and Alcoholism reports the following:

3,000,000 teenagers are estimated to be alcoholics. If you drink before age 15, you have four times the chance to develop alcohol dependence than those who begin at age 21. [31]

In a study of 1877 high school seniors nationwide by Penn State University:

> 32% said they drank mostly for the thrill of it, 15% said they used alcohol to relax, and another 36% said they drank just to experiment. A smaller group, 18% said they drank for multiple reasons, including an inability to deal with frustration or anger. They were more likely to get drunk during the day, possibly during school hours. They also said they got drunk frequently; many had started to drink by sixth grade. [32]

> According to the National Highway Safety Administration, between now (May 3) and graduation, 58 percent of traffic

fatalities are attributed to alcohol-related incidents involving teen drivers during the prom and graduation period. [33]

College and university students have their problems with alcohol, as well. The Center for Science in the Public Interest reports the following:

Forty-four percent of four-year college students drink alcohol at the binge level or higher. Binge level is 5 or more drinks for males or 4 or more for females in a 2 hour period. Forty-eight percent of college drinkers report that "drinking to get drunk" is an important reason for drinking. Almost 1 in 4 drink alcohol 10 or more times a month and twenty-nine percent report getting intoxicated 3 or more times per month. College students who first became intoxicated before age nineteen are more likely to become alcohol dependent and frequent heavy drinkers. 1700 college students are killed each year from alcohol-related accidental injuries. 100,000 students per year report having been too drunk to know whether they consented to have sex or not. College presidents report that binge drinking is the most serious problem on campus. [34]

The National Center on Addiction and Substance Abuse at Columbia University reports the following:

1993 to 2005 increases in college students using other drugs are amazing: opioids (Vicodin and OxyContin) up 343 percent; stimulants (Ritalin and Adderall) up 93 percent; tranquilizers (Xanax and Valium) up 450 percent; sedatives (Nembutal and Seconal) up 225 percent; daily marijuana use up 100 percent; cocaine, heroin and other illegal drugs up 52 percent. 310,000 college students smoke marijuana daily and 636,000 use other illegal drugs (other than marijuana) such as cocaine and heroin. [35]

Over-the-counter cough-suppressing products are becoming the drug of choice among children, teens, and young adults:

But the reality of abusing over-the-counter cough and cold medications can be harsh . . . the active ingredient in many of these products, Dextromethorphan or DXM, can cause comas, seizures, and death in high doses. The National Institute of Drug Abuse sponsored studies said 5 percent of 10th graders, and 7 percent of 12th graders had taken the drugs to get high. Paul Doering, a professor of Pharmacy at the University of Florida, said, "One of the more alarming aspects of the abuse has been the availability of dextromethorphan online."[36]

What about the War on Drugs? Leonard Pitts, writing in the *Florida Times-Union*, says the following:

Jack A. Cole spent 26 years with the New Jersey State Police, with 12 as an undercover narcotics officer. In 2002, he started the organization, Law Enforcement against Prohibition, LEAP, which now has 12,000 members. In 1970, says Cole, 2 percent of the population over age twelve had at some point or another used an illegal drug. As of 2003, he says, that number stood at 46 percent, an increase of "2,300 percent." In 1914, when the first drug law was passed, the government predicted 1.3% of Americans were addicted to illegal drugs. In 1970, the War on Drugs started and addiction was again predicted at 1.3%. With 39,000,000 drug arrests since then, it was still at 1.3%. That is the only statistic that has not changed. Yet, we have spent a trillion dollars and imprisoned more people per capita than any country in the world in order to "reduce drug use." As a conclusion, he suggests it may be time to legalize the use of drugs. [37]

Smoking is also a problem:

> Every day in the United States about 4,000 kids ages 12 to 17 try smoking for the first time. And every day, an estimated 1140 become regular smokers, putting themselves at higher risk of disease and premature death. Tobacco kills 1200 a day. [38]

Obesity among both children and adults is a serious and increasing problem:

> American obesity rates are the highest in the world with 64% of adults being overweight or obese, and 26% are obese. Estimates of the number of obese American adults have been rising steadily, from 19.4 % in 1997, 24.5% in 2004 to 26.6% in 2007. Should current trends continue, 75% of adults in the U. S. are projected to be overweight and 41% obese by 2015. [39]

The obesity rate in children has increased from data for 1976-80 to 2003-06 as follows:

- Children aged 2-5 from 5.0% to 12.4%
- Children aged 6-11 from 6.5% to 17.0%
- Children aged 12-19 from 5.0% to 17.6% [40]

The consequences of obesity are severe according to the surgeon general:

> For adults:

- An estimated 300,000 deaths per year may be attributable to obesity
- 50-100 percent probability of earlier death from all causes
- High blood pressure twice as likely
- 80 percent of diabetics are overweight
- Higher risk of some cancers
- Each two-pound weight gain ups arthritis risk from 9 percent to 13 percent
- Pregnancy obesity related to birth defects like spina bifida
- Higher risk of gall bladder disease, incontinence, depression
- Limited mobility and staying power

For children:

- Increased frequency for heart disease, high blood pressure/cholesterol
- Alarming increase in type 2 diabetes—once known as an adult disease
- Overweight children are 70 percent more likely to become overweight adults
- As perceived by themselves, social discrimination [41]

It is time for adults, children, families, educators, mentors, and health professionals to better reinforce those principles like self-control, moderation, and self-respect that can change factors that influence health:

- reduction in convenience/fast food
- healthful school lunches and drinks
- nutritious breakfasts and home-prepared, sit-down dinners
- less sedentary couch time and much more exercise
- more family time in healthy activity
- family and private parent-to-children discussions about sexual behavior, smoking, and alcohol and drug abuse
- predetermined awards and penalties per the above

Beyond these alarming statistics on specific health care issues, let's take a look at American health care in general. These statistics are based on an analysis and survey of by the Commonwealth Fund of 112,000 adults in Australia, Britain, Canada, Germany, the Netherlands, and New Zealand compared to the United States:

Health care spending in those countries ranged from 8.3% to 10.7% of Gross Domestic Product compared to 16% in the U. S.

Life expectancy ranged from 78.7 to 80.6 years compared to 77.9% in the U. S.

Infant mortality rate per 1,000 births ranged from 4.1% to 5.7% compared to 6.89% in the U. S.

Patients surveyed in those countries as to whether the health care system needs to be rebuilt completely range from 9% to 18%, with Canada at 27% compared to 34% in the U.S.

Patients reporting medical mistakes in the past two years ranged from 16% to 28% compared to 32% in the U. S.

The other six nations spend ½ as much of their GDP on health care as the U.S. [42]

Thirteen million children are living in poverty thereby ranking the United States worst among the 24 wealthiest countries . . . Eight million children have no health insurance. More than 3 million children are reported abused and neglected, and about 1500 children die each year as a result of such abuse and neglect. As many as 14 million children, including an estimated 40,000 kindergartners, are on their own after school. Nearly 2 million children have parents in prison. [43]

The virtues behind the decisions leading to these alarming conclusions about American health care need urgent reappraisal. With sound values in place and commitment to apply them, these conditions can be controlled and improved over time.

The kind of ethics that lead to spousal and child abuse I find difficult to comprehend. How could any sane person who took vows of marriage or shares a life with someone he or she loves or has a close work relationship abuse his or her partner? Even more difficult, how could any sane person abuse a baby or a child? I would define abuse as deliberate, extreme, and sustained emotional, physical, sexual, financial, or stalking actions.

My wife and I have had a good and loving marriage for sixty years. Over those years, we have had many disagreements and arguments. As a fly on the wall who observed only the heat of a particular quarrel, someone might think we were being verbally abusive to each other. While there was some immediate hurt, those disagreements were always very situational, and we both knew we had overreacted and did not really mean the exact words that were said or feelings expressed. Those feelings were soon put aside, and forgiveness prevailed. Calmer discussion usually resolved the situation to both our satisfactions. I am sure most of you have been in similar situations, and that is not abuse. Marriage is not all fun and games—it takes clear virtues about love and commitment and hard work to survive its ups and downs. Sharing, enjoying, recalling the many ups, finding mutual and effective ways to resolve the downs, and growing together from both is what it is all about.

Physical and sexual spousal and child abuse are the result of a severe lack of positive, consistent values. While that abuse declined in the '90s, it is still a major problem. Most all studies suggest actual statistics are much higher than those reported. Following are some conclusions from a number of studies.

Futures Without Violence (formerly the Family Violence Prevention Fund) reports the following:

- Thirty-one percent of American women are sexually abused by a husband or boyfriend at some point in their lives.
- Women account for 85 percent of the victims of intimate partner violence.
- One in five female high school students are physically and/ or sexually abused by a dating partner.
- Fifty percent of the men who frequently assaulted their wives also abused their children. [44]

The Domestic Violence Resource Center reports:

- Women of all races are equally vulnerable to violence by an intimate.
- People with lower annual income (below $25K) are at a 3-times-higher risk of intimate partner violence than people with higher annual income (over $50K).
- On average, more than three women and one man are murdered by their intimate partners in this country every day. [45]

Childhelp reports:

- 3 million child abuse reports are made each year in the U.S.—experts put the actual number three times higher.
- 4 children die every day as a result of child abuse with 3 being under the age of 4.
- 1/3 of abused and neglected children will abuse their own children.
- Abused children are 59% more likely to be arrested as a child, 28% more arrested as an adult, and 30% more likely to commit violent crime. [46]

Bullying is a nationwide problem. According to Bullying Statistics 2010:

> . . . there are about 2.7 million students being bullied each year by about 2.1 million students taking on the role of the bully. Over half, about 56 percent, of all students have witnessed a bullying crime take place while at school. Along that same vein, about one of every 10 students drops out or changes schools because of repeated bullying. There are about 282,000 students that are reportedly attacked in high schools throughout the nation each month. [47]

From the Associated Press: sixteen-year-old Sladjana Vidovic "tied one end of a rope around her neck and the other to a bedpost, before jumping out her bedroom window." Her last note "told of her daily torment at Mentor High School in Ohio where students mocked her accent, taunted her with insults like 'Slutty Jana,' and threw food at her." A boy pushed her down the stairs and she got phone calls late at night telling her to go back to Croatia and she would be dead in the morning. "The family watched as the girls who had tormented Sladjana for months walked up to her casket—and laughed." This was the fourth bullied student in two years in this Cleveland suburb to commit suicide—one was gay, one had a learning disability, and one boy liked to wear pink. Mentor, Ohio, was voted one of the "100 best places to live" by CNN and Money Magazine in 2010. [48]

It is very difficult to imagine how a value system developed in those homes and in their schools, that allowed this to happen. This certainly demonstrates the decline in most basic morals even in this supposedly tranquil community.

Commitment: Marriage, Divorce, Cohabitation, Single Parenthood

Marriage rates are falling, and cohabitation (man and woman living together unmarried) and single-parent relationships are increasing.

The latest census data show the share of households with married couples fell below 50% for the first time. [49]

Unmarried (cohabiting) couple households without children increased from less than 1 million in 1980 to 4 million in 2010 and with children from less than 1 million in 1980 to almost 3 million in 2010 according to the U.S. Census Bureau. [50]

There were 13.7 million single mothers in 2009 raising 26 percent of the children in the U.S. compared to 12 percent in 1970 as reported by Net Industries. [51]

Even today, those writing about marriage and cohabitation cite data from a comprehensive report by the National Survey of Family Growth in 2002. Interviews held with 12,571 adults, including 7,463 females and 4,928 males from ages 15 to 44, showed the following:

Married persons have better mental and physical health, live longer, and have lower rates of cardiovascular disease than unmarried persons.

Children born to unmarried mothers have more critical risk for poverty, teen childbearing, poor school achievement, and marital disruption in adulthood than children born to married mothers. [52]

A Pew Research Center report says this about fathers:
Forty-six percent of fathers age 15 to 44 had at least one child outside their marriage. That compares well to government data showing the share of babies born to unwed mothers went from 5 percent in 1960 to 41 percent in 2008.

Twenty-seven percent of fathers with children 18 or younger live away from at least one of their children.

Black fathers have children out of wedlock at 72 percent, Hispanics at 59 percent and whites at 37 percent.

Thirteen percent of fathers with a bachelor's degree had children outside marriage compared to 51 percent with high school diplomas and 65 percent for those that did not finish high school. [53]

The *Atlanta Journal Constitution* reports the following:

> Early marriage is a key predictor of later divorce. Nearly half of people who marry under age 18 and 40 percent under age 20 end up divorced. It's only 24 percent for people who marry after age 25. [54]

Dr. Bill Maier of Focus on Family reports the following:

The percentage of high school seniors who feel it is okay to live together before marriage has increased from 35 percent in 1975 to 60 percent in 2001. [55]

Dr. Patrick Schneider summarizes some of the problems with out-of-marriage cohabitation as reported in other studies.

The Broken Hearth by W. J. Bennett:

> The rate of divorce among those who cohabit prior to marriage is nearly double (39 percent vs. 21 percent) that of couples who marry without cohabitation.

A presentation by J. C. Crouse:

> Men in cohabiting relationships are four times more likely to be unfaithful than husbands.

T. Drake of the *National Catholic Register:*

> Seventy percent of juveniles in state-operated institutions (prisons) are from fatherless homes. [56]

A recent editorial in the *Florida Times-Union* takes this position:

"The basic foundations of American life are in jeopardy with a growing decline in marriage among the middle class." This trend was caused by: permissive attitudes—more acceptance of divorce and premarital sex; more risky behaviors—multiple sexual partners and infidelity; the decline of middle-class values—such as gratification. "Can American society thrive without thriving marriages? This is an experiment we don't want to attempt." [57]

Each adult facing a relationship, love, and the future must make sure that sound and positive principles are driving his or her choices: traditional marriage without cohabitation, cohabitation with a commitment to marriage, or cohabitation with hope that it will work.

Both parties need the same commitment.

Responsibility

Too many organizations and individuals do not have the proper sense of responsibility and accountability for what they do and its impact on themselves, those they influence, and society. Looking at what some people get paid for what they do is a good place to start:

Chief executive compensation grew 275 times to that of the average worker's income by 2007—up from 25 times in 1965. Looked at in another way, that equates to the CEO having to work 3 hours to earn what a lower paid worker earns for the full year. The CEOs in the Standard & Poor's 500 stock index earned over $4,000 per hour. [58]

National Football League median salaries went from $482,000 in 2000 to $850,000 in 2008. This does not include signing bonuses and endorsements. San Francisco had the high median at $1,325,000 with St. Louis low at $488,000. Major League Baseball average salaries went from $513,000 in 1989 to $3,298,000 in 2008. This includes signing bonuses. National Basketball Association average salaries were about $5,000,000 for 2007-08. This does not include endorsements. [59]

Employees of Wall Street pure investment banks take home 60% of their firms' revenue as compensation. This excessive Wall Street bonus system has led to "swashbuckling" decision making as far as leveraging, borrowing, and short-term greed versus long-term stability and growth. [60]

Unfortunately, in too many of the situations above, the compensation of some involved is in no way proportional to their results and contribution. We should not be concerned with the compensation of an executive who leads a firm that has quality products, puts his employees and customers first, consistently grows revenue and profits, expands its American workforce, increases the rewards to investors, pays appropriate wages and taxes, is a positive community and environmental force, and abides by rules and legalities in place. Any employees who perform at or above the norms for their positions should receive reasonable and competitive pay, benefits, and appropriate incentives. We do not mind the pay of an athlete who produces outstanding results in his or her sport, who fills stadiums, is a team leader, and is a positive role model for others. We do not mind the pay of a Wall Street trader that puts the customer first and whose actions are legal and conservative and enhance long-term economic and financial value. We do not mind the pay of an actor, actress, or entertainer who performs brilliantly and exceeds the expectations of the audience. We choose what companies' products to buy, what sporting events to attend, and what performances to see. That is quite different from what the recent financial and Wall Street crowd did. They made decisions that often stretched legality into fraud and contributed to a financial and housing disaster that negatively affected our entire nation. Most of us were unaware of what was going on and had no choice in the outcomes. For the financial industry, we need better controls to see that the customer and society are protected and that this cannot happen again. And, those controls must do that while not destroying financial industry innovation in the process.

State and city governments are no less guilty when it comes to values like responsibility.

The Kellogg School of Management at Northwestern University and the University of Rochester report: "An unfunded liability of about $5,300 per worker—with the total estimate at $574 billion for all local governments in the U.S." San Diego is a good example. Elected officials allowed workers to dramatically spike their pre-retirement compensation to retire on more than 100% of their pay, and to draw both their salaries and pensions simultaneously. A city worker, qualifying for retirement, can instead remain on the job and receive both his salary and an early activated pension which is deposited in an account earning an annual 8% rate of interest and cost of living adjustment. While sweetening the pay/pension pot each year, the city council has underfunded the plan, as recommended by its actuary, for a decade. It is now short by $1.1 billion which the taxpayers will have to pony up. The pension benefits are constitutionally mandated by California law and the same is true in 40 other states. This is typical of the situation in many localities around the country leading to the huge deficit which tax payers will probably have to make up. [61]

I am sure most of you, along with me, wonder how this could happen. The ethics of many politicians allowed them to avoid negotiating tough issues and remain happy doling out lush benefits to heavily unionized employees during good and bad economic times in a system that somehow lets them push the costs for those increased benefits off on future generations. And, we—as the general public—were just not paying attention and will pay the bill or the consequences of potentially bankrupt and failed governments.

The values which guide standards of excellence in the schools that educate our teachers are missing. The Education Schools Project reports the following:

> Three-quarters of America's 1206 university-level schools of education don't have the capacity to produce excellent teachers. More than half of teachers are educated in programs with the lowest admission standards (often 100% acceptance rates) and 'the least accomplished professors.' When school principals were asked to rate the skills of new teachers only 40% on average thought education schools were doing even a moderately good job. [62]

Subtle racial prejudice values embedded into our brains are difficult to get rid of even when carefully tested. A study by the University of Chicago and MIT reports the following:

"Researchers sent thousands of fictitious resumes to large corporations." The resumes were identical except for the names attached to them. "Some sounded black (La Toya, Lakisha, Jamal); some sounded white (Brendan, Emily, Daniel)." The white-name resumes were two times as likely to be called for an interview as the black-sounding ones. "If they are typical, many of the recruiters were supposed to be actively seeking qualified people of color." Their decisions came out of a largely unconscious reaction to names. "The recruiters were both white and black." All discriminated against names that sounded black. [63]

Many baby boomers did not think enough about the proper balance between the values behind "live for today" and "future well-being and financial independence." They lived well in the good times and did not save enough to cover the current bad times. The Associated Press writes the following:

"The situation is extremely serious because baby boomers have not saved very effectively for retirement and are still retiring too early," says Olivia Mitchell, director of the Boettner Center for Pensions and Retirement research at the University of Pennsylvania. "Michael Vanatta, 61, of Vero Beach, is paying the price of being a boomer who enjoyed life without saving for the future. It's my fault. For years I was making plenty of money and spending plenty of money." Vanatta is typical of the majority. Fifty-one percent of early boomer households, aged 55 to 64, face a retirement with living standards lower than they are used to. By far the biggest cause has been a failure to save. [64]

Moral Character

"Moral" is knowing the difference between right and wrong and striving to be right. As far as values, that means one must have a clear understanding of honesty, trust, and loyalty versus dishonesty, lack of trust, and disloyalty. In today's world, changes in lifestyles, pressures to excel, reward structures, needs for acceptance, and economic survival provide ample temptations to blur those moral codes and thus also blur the distinction between what is right and what is wrong. Only you can decide your course. Do a cost-benefit analysis, and honestly evaluate gratification and gain over risks. Think through both the short and long term. If you succumb, check frequently to make sure the immediate gains still outweigh the consequences. If they don't get out of that situation, take your lumps, and get on with your life. Either that or fade away to a lonely, narrow, and meaningless existence.

In today's media-driven world, there are many ways to be tempted. Katherine Kersten writes the following in the *Minneapolis Star Tribune*:

Pharrell Williams is a rapper musician and icon of the youth culture. The Grammy Award he won in 2007 for "Money Maker" was so saturated with lyrics of sex, vulgarity, and degradation that the writer for this newspaper could not print them. These are excerpts from the Grammy nominated song "Drop It Like It's Hot" with rapper Snoop Dog. It begins with a gun, shooting, and cement shoes and ends:

> Your family's crying, now you on the news
> They can't find you, and now they miss you
> Must I remind you I'm only here to twist you
> Pistol whip you, dip you, then flip you.

Williams summed up his worldview to the *Minneapolis Star Tribune* by saying he does what he wants to do and wants you to do the same. That's what makes an individual. Most will not, "but some in our society will take the idea to its logical conclusion." [65]

Hostility toward religion has reached a new level.

"As he presented a folded flag to a widow, a civilian member of an honor guard at a national veterans' cemetery uttered the words: 'God bless you and this family and God bless the United States of America.' The blessing was requested by the family. However, two other honor guards complained—and the man, a Vietnam combat veteran, was fired." His supervisor said he not only broke protocol, but made a hostile work environment. "To deny comfort to a grieving family at a veteran's grave site is merely cruelty in the name of political correctness." [66]

What kind of value supports that?

The publicity and availability of soft and not-so-soft pornography may not create just a one-time or short-term temptation to positive moral beliefs of youth and adults. In a *Viewpoint* editorial, Mona Charen of Creators Syndicate makes this point:

"We all know how far the pornification has gotten." Hotels have pornographic films and leave the film name off the bill. Victoria's Secret is on TV and not very secret. Viagra is presented often in magazines and on TV. "Television, music videos, and magazines at supermarket checkout counters contain the kinds of words and images that once would have been considered soft porn. "800 million pornographic videos and DVDs are rented each year. Men look at them online more than anything else. Of course, only people with strange sexual drives are drawn to this, right? Not exactly. One psychiatrist feels that pornography alters the mind of users. "Like other addictions, pornography use breeds tolerance and the need for more intensity to get the desired results. [67]

We are all aware that examples of pornography abuses that involve well-known people in many fields are in the headlines. Political figures rise to the top.

Congressman Anthony Weiner, married and a democrat from Queens, admitted sending sexually suggestive photos (including a man's crotch) and messages to 6 women online over 3 years. He also admitted that initially he had lied to cover up his actions. He also said he would not resign from Congress but would get treatment. With increasing pressure he has resigned. [68]

Pornography is not acceptable if it hard wires values that make its increasing use and potentially serious outcomes a general lifestyle. My moral code certainly includes earned forgiveness. But sometimes, I feel our permissive-value flexibility has taken forgiveness so far that it has made the serious acts that caused it trivial. They should not be forgotten, but they seem to be.

- President Clinton has full honors to represent America as a worldwide goodwill ambassador even with his code of behavior leading to sexual exploits in the Oval Office while president of the United States.
- Elliot Spitzer had a CNN public talk show even with his ethics leading to promiscuity with a call girl while in a trusted position in New York State. Spitzer was bounced from CNN after less than a year.

Thus, it is interesting to ponder the future reputation of those like ex-Congressman Weiner along with the ex-governor of California Arnold Schwarzenegger. I also wonder what the impact of their actions could be on the value development and acceptable behavior of our young people?

A few other miscellaneous conditions needing a values-and-results review follow.

More than 40 percent of dads do not read to their children. [69]

In 1967, one in seven Americans lived in poverty, while today that rate is one in eight. [70]

Black families have to work the equivalent of twelve more weeks to earn the same annual income as white families. [71]

About one-third of sixty-four million American Catholics never attend mass, and the younger generation considers religion important, but doesn't equate faith with going to church. [72]

One in four Americans, aged 18-29, claim no religious affiliation. Survey consultant Roger Funk says, "Right now, there is a dropping confidence in organized religion, especially in the traditional religious forums." [73]

From 1997 to 2003, there was a 50 percent drop in kids who participated in outdoor activities, such as walking, hiking, and fishing, according to a University of Maryland study. The Nature Conservancy found that kids under thirteen now take part in freestyle play outdoors for only one half hour per week. [74]

More than twelve thousand homicides by gun were reported in 2005 with wounded at fifty-three thousand for 2006. Lifetime costs to the country are estimated at over seven billion. [75]

One in four teenage girls has a sexually transmitted disease. [76]

Average 2010 credit card debt for households having credit card debt is $15,788. [77]

The United States is the world's leading jailer: per 100,000 population, there are 750 in jail; for Russia, 600; for South Africa, 325; for Europe, 140; for Canada, 100; for Australia, 125; for Japan, 75. [78]

African-American men are nearly twelve times more likely to be imprisoned for drug convictions than whites. [79]

The World Hunger Education Service reports that there has been a dramatic increase in hunger in the United States in the three years, 2008, 2009, 2010. Statistics are only available for 2008. They show seventeen million households, 14.6 percent of households, were food insecure—the highest number ever recorded in the United States. [80]

Who's Who has long been the nation's premier biographical reference for VIP persons. One-third of 333 persons whose profiles stated they earned one of the nation's most esteemed military medals cannot be affirmed by military records. [81]

Somewhere behind each of these examples lies a breakdown in sound and positive values. We should not rationalize these outcomes by letting our ethics and morals adapt to fit the situation. I hope most Americans would not want the *intent* of the values that made this country great changed or allowed to float—virtues like those expressed in the Ten Commandments, the Golden Rule, along with commitment, hard work, moderation, self-determination and improvement, pride in accomplishment, service to nation, local community responsibility, and importance of family. We do need to think carefully about how to and whether to *reinterpret* values that are being abused, not well applied, not applied equally to all segments of society, or are not supportive or are in conflict with beneficial changes in technology and societal living.

I believe a fair analogy is our United States Constitution. Again, I would hope most all Americans would not want the basic intent of its principles to change. Careful thought must be given as to how to reinterpret and apply those constitutional principles that have been abused, not applied equally to all, or require new interpretation for significant changes in technology, lifestyle, or social patterns. But there are significant differences between how those constitutional principles are reinterpreted and protected compared to the general values that guide our lives and society. As far as the Constitution is concerned, specific checks and balances are in place. Either congressional legislation or challenges from individuals or groups coming up through the courts begin that reinterpretation. While that is well debated along the way, ultimately, the Supreme Court decides whether it is changing constitutional intent and negates or supports it.

Beyond the law, there are no such built-in checks and balances on how our general societal values get reinterpreted and the resulting outcomes. Free will is in place. Of course, change is important and constant. Women should be allowed to vote and be paid equally to men for equal work. Black people should not have to ride in the back of the bus or be limited in where they may stay, eat, or be educated. But today, what often seems missing as societal change takes place is the application of a sound moral or ethical filter. The best assurance that this filter is in place is a clear conscience and God's blessing.

As I review this chapter, too many of America's positive and time-tested values are being applied in ways that are close to tipping their intent in the wrong direction. If the results from these changes continue to become our general way of life, I believe our country is on the slippery slope from greatness to mediocrity to _____. You can fill in the blank.

Some excerpts from George Carlin's writings provide a challenging and thoughtful summary for this chapter. We have:

- taller buildings, but shorter tempers
- wider freeways, but narrower viewpoints
- spend more, but have less
- buy more, but enjoy less
- bigger houses and smaller families
- more conveniences, but less time

51

- more degrees, but less sense
- more knowledge, but less judgment
- more experts, yet more problems
- more medicine, but less wellness
- multiplied our possessions, but reduced our values
- love too seldom, and hate too often
- learned how to make a living, but not a life
- added years to life, not life to years
- cleaned up the air, but polluted the soul
- conquered the atom, but not our prejudice
- learned to rush, but not to wait
- big men and small character
- steep profits and shallow relationships
- two incomes, but more divorce
- fancier houses but broken homes [82]

You may not agree with all the conclusions in this chapter. And we can all cite positive results to some outcomes. But I hope you would be in support of three points. First, the primary cause of those results—that were good but are now not so good—is our failure to continue to apply those values which made them good in the first place. Second, those outcomes, which never were acceptable and stayed that way, will only be improved by a committed application of those same values. Third, and most important, *we have the power to make a difference!*

Let's see how we do it. To begin the process, we need to understand how our values develop and are applied.

Chapter 2

THE ORIGIN OF VALUES

I tend to look on the brighter side of any situation I face, and therefore, as *Free Merriam-Webster Dictionary* defines it, I am an optimist. Of course, no one bats 1.000. In my life, some situations did not turn out for the best, and some were failures. I made lots of mistakes, including:

- not thinking or working hard enough;
- at times, working or playing when I should have been doing something else;
- being tempted by immediate gratification;
- youthful experimentation; and
- being influenced by others or events I did not control.

But I know, in looking back, that my batting average would have been a lot lower without the basic values I grew up with.

I am using my life to show how values develop for two reasons. First, because I experienced it, it is my clearest way to illustrate what values are, how they develop along the way, how they guide life in terms of what went well, and mistakes along the way. Second, it will give you a format and a story line to think back over your life and how your values developed and were applied. This is essential preparation for chapters 3 and 4.

I was fortunate to grow up with loving parents, outstanding public education, and with close and responsible friends in a safe, small community. I went to college, have been married to a wonderful woman for six decades, helped raise four great sons (my wife gets most of the credit), and enjoyed a busy and satisfying career. Now, Charlotte and I enjoy retirement, our four sons and their wives and our twelve grandchildren, good friends, travel, hobbies, volunteer activities, community events, Florida winters, and Minnesota summers. My values were developed and then shaped and applied at each stage in my life. They guided my decision making, behavior, and relationships with others at each exciting, positive, and rewarding phase of my life.

At an early age, my grandfather, who had been a carpenter and contractor, taught me about tools and the value of accuracy and patience to produce quality that would show and last. My little five-foot-tall grandmother ran my six-foot-tall grandfather's home life in a positive, gracious, and firm way. There was a classic family saying that came from my grandmother and was used when anyone went a little too far: "Grandpa doesn't want any more mashed potatoes." From her, I initially learned the value of caring for others and that stature and strength are not required to do that.

My father was doing well selling life insurance until the crash of 1929. While few were buying insurance, there were no other jobs, so he struggled on in the insurance business. We were poor but always had a roof over our heads and food on the table. My father was too proud to give in to federal work programs, such as the Works Progress Administration (WPA) or the Civilian Conservation Corps (CCC). From him, I learned the values of self-determination, pride, and hard work, even under very adverse circumstances.

We moved seven times by the time I was twelve. To reduce expenses, we lived with my older sister and her husband. While I felt good about our close family relationship, I decided to do all I could not to be poor. I added the value of working smart to working hard. In my early teens, I worked hard to earn an extra-big paper route, which I covered on my bike. I was a caddy on weekends at the country club where we worked thirty-six holes each day carrying double leather bags. It was hard work, and it kept me from other fun activities, but the $1.30 per day for the paper route and the five dollars a day for caddying kept me in spending money, helped the family coffers a little, and put me in with other youngsters with similar values and expectations.

I was brought up in a Christian home. I went to Sunday school and joined the church. I found my values were enhanced and expanded by what I learned from the Golden Rule, the Ten Commandments and other principles from the Bible, my teachers, and my minister. It was an okay place to spend Sunday morning, seated among dedicated people and hearing good things. But as a young boy, I don't think the depth and true meaning of being a Christian really took hold. It was enough just hearing about positive values and then trying to lead a good life.

My father traveled a lot, and while he fully supported her, it was my mother who added the most to the values I carry today. From her, I first learned the value of giving to others, and that is one big part of love. My mother dedicated her life and love to her family. I know that her devotion kept my father's spirit alive during those tough times. She was the peacemaker between my father and her daughter from a previous marriage. She always kindly accepted his irritability from a very painful stomach ulcer. On top of that, as she raised me, too often I did not make that easy. Looking back, I am afraid that, in too many instances, I learned the relevance of sound values from her by having strayed from them. From my experiences with friends, I learned that the normal testing of boundaries did not work so well without sound values to begin with.

My mother had the virtue of patience, and I certainly tested it! She knew about positive reinforcement before it was invented. She praised my accomplishments but, in good ways, said how I could do better. I shared problems, and she always made me think through how to attack them. She knew my friends well and spent lots of time with them in our home. From her, I learned about appropriate praise for things well done and thoughtful counseling when problems arose. She added much to my ethic of hard work—good things do not come easy but are worth going after. She, as well as my father, never harshly punished me. Rather, they let me figure out that they knew when my behavior was improper and thus let me punish myself.

I learned about integrity. For example, during the earlier good times, my parents purchased a houseful of quality furniture, mainly on credit. During the bad times, I remember their struggles to pay back every cent on that furniture, month by month, in small amounts.

During high school, and later at the University of Tennessee, I was on the swimming team. From that, I learned a little about being humble in victory and gracious in defeat. I still struggle to consistently apply the virtue of being gracious in defeat to this day. During my junior and senior years in high school and the first two years of college, I worked summers full time and part time during school at an International Harvester iron foundry. From that experience, I learned about character at a very basic blue-collar working level. As all pay was based on piecework at fifty cents per ton of iron handled, I learned that hard work paid off. I earned over one hundred dollars per week and not only saved a lot but had an economic lifestyle above most of my peers. That was more money than a lot of adults earned. I learned much about honesty, teamwork, and the good, tired feelings from hot and sweat-laden hard work. I also learned that I did not want to spend my working life in the foundry.

While I did not realize it at the time, I learned that ethnic differences made no difference to the work environment and to my life. Along with older whites, there were many Italians and Mexicans, along with huge black men brought in from the Caribbean to replace our young men who were off fighting World War II. The Italian men were small but strong. They brought in jars of homemade food, which they heated on the annealing ovens. Sharing that put my sandwiches to shame. I worked as a team with a huge Mexican man named Pancho. While we shared piecework pay, he carried more of the load when we unloaded heavy castings from the hot ovens. Most of these men were not well educated, and I helped them with time cards, load weight tickets, and the like. This made me, as a sixteen-year-old kid, a part of their working camaraderie. Once in a while, I was invited to their homes for real Italian dinners and homemade wine. It was a rough-and-tough environment and, over my four years there, I learned much about the importance of down-to-earth values that I carry today.

I began my college experience at Carroll College (now Carroll University) in Waukesha, Wisconsin. As it was my hometown, I knew all the "spots," and my grades suffered badly. I let good educational and career objectives get overshadowed by short-term social fun. From that, I learned to think about what happens to the application of good principles whenever inevitable temptations come along. I saw that the hometown environment was a major culprit, and so, in the fall of 1949, my best friend Jim Moore and I went off to the University of Tennessee and enrolled as juniors. We quickly learned that some, a small but vocal minority from the South, still carried Civil War values and acted on them when "Yankees" showed up. Values that are hard wired into the brain are difficult to change—more on that later.

My industrial management business major was hard work but enjoyable, and my grades significantly improved. For the first time in college, I saw the relationship between organized study and preparation and pride and accomplishment. It made me wish I could have my Carroll College experience over. But the greatest accomplishment of my years at Tennessee was meeting, dating, and falling in love with my future wife, Charlotte. After sixty years of marriage, I can truly say that it was a fabulous stroke of luck to choose Tennessee, to meet her on a blind date, and to have her accept me as a lifetime partner.

That did not come about easily or the way we would have wanted it to happen. I was a brash, independent, quasi-religious, fun-loving, beer-drinking, and confident—if not cocky—young man . . . and a Yankee to boot. Charlotte's father was a deeply religious, conservative, nondrinking, family-loving, daughter-protecting Southern gentleman and a very successful executive. I was a kid still testing the boundaries while he was a mature adult with a very successful work, family, and community life. I felt the good values I possessed would lead me in the same direction. We got along fine while Charlotte and I were dating, but when it got more serious—and we became engaged—things changed. He began really testing me, as was his right. I was always courteous to him, but I decided not to play games and to let him understand me as I was and wanted to be. I thought that was the right approach. His probing of me centered on my current lifestyle with little concern for the sound values I was testing and my goals for the future. He obviously had concerns about his daughter's future with me. I clearly resented some of his probing, and I am afraid it showed in some of my responses to him. But I was unwilling to tell him what he wanted to hear even if untrue. This severe test of my values convinced me that, while I strayed quite a bit as a young student, good values were in place and would guide my future with Charlotte in positive directions. As I neared graduation, he strongly suggested we have some time apart to test our love and to wait two years for marriage, until Charlotte graduated. That was a reasonable position for him to take.

In judging the intent of his questions, I did not believe he would ever accept me. He did not like my lifestyle, thought I would never "grow up," and felt that I would never be good enough for his daughter. Charlotte and I were in love, and we agonized considerably about her father's position. After much soul searching, we decided to elope. I graduated in August 1951. Charlotte flew to Wisconsin, and we were married on August 28.

Her father and I never saw each other again. I wish he had accepted me and our marriage. He died in his sixties. Had he lived longer, and seen more of our lives together, perhaps he would have changed his outlook. While we will never know what might have happened had we waited, I believe our decision not to wait was correct. I hope, as he looks down, he sees that we truly love and take care of each other, have a wonderful marriage, have raised four sons with loving wives, and have twelve grandchildren, all of whom are morally, mentally, and physically sound. We worked hard to make our values, lifestyle, work ethic, marriage, and family make him proud. And that helped make our marriage even stronger.

I had two dollars when we got married. My folks gave us enough money and lent us their car to enjoy a weekend honeymoon at a nearby city. My parents immediately accepted Charlotte for the good and loving person she was. We grew up in a hurry. We settled in Madison, Wisconsin, and I began work on an MBA at the university in the fall. My wonderful wife, who never had needed to work, got a clerical job at the downtown library making $185 per month. Between that and my part-time job building a professor's cement block boathouse, we got by. Fortunately, ground beef was three pounds for one dollar. We had a laugh when, as a last resort, she made hamburger soup. We had a one-room "apartment" in a professor's home with the bath down the hall. My folks visited some weekends. I recall that Char baked a cherry pie—her first. The crust was like shoe leather, and my father, bless him, ate his whole slice.

Between two lakes, Madison is frigid in the winter with temperatures down to thirty-five degrees below zero. I found the long walk to school cold and freezing. How my Southern wife walked to the bus each day and waited, I will never know, except when she makes up her mind, she can do it.

We learned much about frugality, sharing, hard work, commitment, and what real love is all about. We often look back and recall that those were—among many—some of the closest and best times in

59

our long married life. Our love, values, hopes, and plans for the future carried us through these early years.

I received my MBA and started on a PhD. I worked part time as an industrial engineer at Oscar Mayer & Company and as a teaching assistant at Wisconsin. Along with Char's job, that increased our income a little. She became pregnant, and we moved to a run-down, three-room apartment with a bath. Well, sort of—the toilet was a pull chain with the tank at the ceiling. We shared the first floor with another couple who had to walk through part of our apartment to get to theirs. Our son John came along, the PhD ended, and I went to work.

Again, my beliefs were honed and extended by Charlotte. My wife is shy but is in no way weak. When she takes a position, I listen, because she is most often right. She values truth and integrity very highly. I remember how often she said to our boys as they grew up, "If you tell me the truth, I will always believe, trust, and support you, but if you lie to me, it will take lots of truth to bring you back to full trust." She values fair argument when appropriate, and I am still learning how better to do that. She has a deep faith in some inherent goodness in almost everyone and every situation that is far stronger than mine. I only recall one person she ever completely disrespected, and that was a woman who did not treat her mother well. Char has a unique ability to handle any personal, family, or relationship problem or issue and finds a way to accept whatever the outcome in a positive way. She does not hold grudges, and it takes a lot for her to lose faith in a friend. She is not aggressive, but when something is important to her, she usually finds ways to make things happen to her liking. And that's fine because the outcome is almost always good. You can see that my values were much extended and enhanced through her. I know, deep in my soul, that without her and my mother's early influence, my life would not have succeeded, and I would have probably settled for mediocrity or worse.

Char's mother and I became good friends, and we shared many enjoyable times. She had an unshakable religious faith and the values that came from it. I respected that very much and tried to add that to my own values. I have made progress but am nowhere near her level. She was outgoing and gave to her community in many ways. She had a way with words, was a skillful writer and publisher, and was fun to talk with and share life experiences. She was kind to and thoughtful of her wide circle of friends and devoted to her heritage and her family. She was so proud of Knoxville—nothing quite equaled her city and Tennessee. I grew to respect and love her very much, and my values were enriched by knowing her.

After graduate school, I worked for Pillsbury as an industrial engineer and a production supervisor. I learned a little about leadership and the importance of sound beliefs in decisions dealing with the issues of a varied workforce with a strong union. Then, I had an opportunity to move to headquarters in Minneapolis, and I became corporate training manager. I was doing well, but my values around drive, ambition, and self-determination caused me to realize it would take many years at my age—and in a large company—to reach a level where I could really impact major strategic and operational decisions. I had always wanted to be with a small, developing firm.

So, at age thirty-two, I left Pillsbury with an opportunity to join a young, three-person start-up consulting firm in Santa Monica, California, called Kepner-Tregoe and Associates (including me, there were only two associates). Our business was installing rational thinking into the management of a client organization. At the time, it seemed like a perfect opportunity with a lot of risk. Bless my good wife. When we discussed leaving my secure job with Pillsbury and joining a new, tiny consulting firm operating in California—whose owners hoped they could pay me—she said, "It is what you have wanted to do. Go for it." It again demonstrated her sense of character and support for me, as we had four little boys, our first house with a mortgage, and very little in the bank. So, I left the family in a Minnesota winter and went off to California for eight weeks.

We built that company into a worldwide consulting firm with a staff of three hundred. That was exciting, challenging, rewarding, and fun, and it took the best of our creative ability, hard work, and collective values. Even at our young ages, with limited experience but entrepreneurial passion, we believed in the importance of sound basic beliefs to guide our strategic and operational decisions. We made some early values visible.

- Transfer our decision-making processes to the clients rather than being paid for suggesting decisions to them.
- See that the clients received useful and practical results from our relationship.
- Our ideas are culture free and valuable to companies and employees around the world.
- Global, far-flung companies need a common language to effectively solve problems and make decisions.
- Growth in revenue and profits are essential to survive and remain independent.
- Our employees should share in the profits from the business.
- Strive to promote from within, but bring in outside talent as our growth requires.
- Support and encourage diversity.

Two major situations stand out as lessons. Our ethical standards suggested that the growth and survival of the firm required long-term decisions and investment. That was troublesome to some members of the firm who focused on their annual profit-sharing bonus.

First, our product was a set of proprietary problem-solving and decision-making processes, which we installed through workshops with the management of large corporations. Our business was well received, and it grew rapidly in the United States, almost faster than we could hire associates to deliver the service. Two of our basic beliefs stated these processes were culture free and were valuable to employees and companies around the world. So, we decided to invest and take our ideas abroad. That decision was also supported by our large international clients. In those early days, there were just a few of us, and that decision almost split the organization in two. My boss Ben Tregoe and I supported that position, while others said, "Why should we invest our time and risk our bonus money overseas when we have all the business we can handle right here?" It was not easy living with those feelings as we invested in that overseas business. But it was well worth it. In a few years, our overseas business was half our revenue and profit. Tough economic times in one area tended to be offset by good economic times in other areas.

Second, in those early days with just a few of us, there was a lot of professional and personal camaraderie, respect, and social friendship among us—a "one-for-all-and-all-for-one" spirit. Some in the organization felt that spirit was really important and could be maintained only if we grew slowly, kept our ideas proprietary, and stayed small in the number of quality associates. But at that same time, our largest client was saying to us, "These ideas have been of real value to our senior management, but now we want to provide them to our fifteen thousand supervisory employees." We could not have hired and trained enough associates to accomplish that for years out. It was, however, an opportunity that supported our belief and passion that these ideas were needed by everyone, and we had to work it out, even with mixed feelings in the firm.

So, we created a licensing approach where we trained and certified carefully selected client employees to deliver our ideas to those larger populations based on fees and royalties to us. Again, some associates felt strongly that, while this alternative could produce rapid growth, we would lose our close spirit, as well as the proprietary position and value of our ideas. That decision and delivery method soon spread across many of the clients and produced significant growth and profit for the firm over time.

Following our basic beliefs in those two instances created the future for our business. When it came to integrating sound personal and business values and consistently applying them to decision making, my boss, colleague, and friend Dr. Benjamin Tregoe was my mentor. The examples above well illustrate that point. I worked closely for and with him over my career of thirty-five years. We not only applied those values to our existing business but also made basic beliefs central to a strategy formulation process we developed during the 1980s and published as *Top Management Strategy*. [1] We applied that process with senior management of major clients around the world over the next twenty years. From Ben, my values about the discipline of hard work, integrity, trust, passion, commitment, loyalty, pride in accomplishment, perseverance, true friendship, and respect were significantly enhanced and hard wired to my life.

Throughout my career, I was fortunate to work with many executives, managers, and employees of major companies across the world. They saw the long-term benefits for consistently applying their organization's sound and positive code of conduct as part of their business decisions, behavior, and relationships with others. I got to know several of those executives beyond business and saw that their personal values squared quite well with their business values. I learned that their beliefs were the cornerstone of their personal, family, and community life. These were good people, and I know they slept well most every night.

All of those consulting experiences reinforced my dedication to the critical importance of having positive ethical and moral principles to guide both my business and personal life. Beyond that, I saw the need to share those principles with others. I, too, slept well most every night.

There are always temptations along the way that could cause one to compromise or ignore a sound value. Those tempting situations always seem to provide enough immediate gratification to mask consideration of longer-term consequences. I recall an early Sunday school experience. We did not have a lot, but my folks always gave me a dime for the collection. On my walk to the church, I passed a corner grocery that had a large penny candy counter. So, in a weak moment, I stopped and spent a nickel of that Sunday school money on candy. It was good, and I did that several times. Finally, my conscience and ethics took over, and I stopped. Guilt is a most powerful motivator to get a person back on a sound path. That memory still helps me whenever I am confronted with minor temptations, such as filling out expense reports, recording golf scores, telling fish stories, reporting income taxes, and the like.

In high school, the choir was asked to sing at a downtown social club meeting over the lunch hour. Several choir friends and I decided to skip our boring history class after lunch and go to the drugstore and drink sodas. So, we snuck out on the walk back. Of course, we got caught. Our punishment was to sand off all the initials and graffiti carved over time in the wooden desktops in that history classroom and refinish them. I do not recall the exact number of hours after school it took, but it was enough that we vowed never again to let our value about this kind of conduct be further tempted.

My last quarter at Tennessee was extremely difficult. I was carrying over twenty credit hours so I could graduate on time. One course I found boring was Business Law. I did not like it and fell way behind in homework and quizzes. A "friend" told me he could buy the answers to the true-false/multiple-choice final exam for ten dollars. I succumbed to the temptation and bought the answers, all of which I memorized. At final exam time came the consequences. Because I had not studied, I had no idea how hard the test would be for those who had studied. I still remember breaking out in a sweat as I faced the dilemma. If I got too many answers right—beyond those good students who had studied—the professor would smell a rat. If I got too many wrong answers—below those who had studied—I would fail and not graduate. Somehow, I found the right balance and ended up with a B for the course. I decided that cheating was not worth the stress it caused and that honesty and hard work would be better guidelines for my future.

I was fortunate to be raised in a family with sound and positive values and to have friends, teachers, and mentors who encouraged the application of those beliefs in all the many situations that confronted me in growing up. That kept my youthful value transgressions at a relatively minor level, kept me from serious trouble, and put my adult life on a fairly sound track.

As a summary to this life scenario, these are the basic values which I try hard to apply to my life. I say "try" because I am in no way perfect and am conscious of the need to improve. They are as follows:

- Hard work makes life worthwhile.
- Think and question before you act; be smart.
- Use your brains and talents to their fullest extent.
- Trust is vital to a meaningful life and earned over time through actions.
- Be honest, truthful, and have integrity; tell it like it is.
- Give back to others, and share of yourself what you have been given.
- Seek, find, and then do what you are the best at and be optimistic in what you do.
- Immediate gains from a breakdown in values are never worth the consequences.
- Never stop learning, and seek new challenges; you can always improve and grow.
- Live below your standard of living, tomorrow will soon be here.
- Seek and care about others' views and feelings—both when you agree and when you don't.
- Achieving a loving and responsible family is worth anything it takes.
- Be conscious of your values as a guide for any decision you make, your behavior, and your relationships with others.

My wife shares those values and applied them well while raising our children and to her life. With my travel schedule, she had the primary day-by-day responsibility for their behavior and development.

This is how my values and beliefs developed and were applied. I tried to include enough detail so you could find parallels, similarities, or differences in your values and life experiences. It is inspirational to look back once in a while and determine what made your life what it is. You will find that your values were a key part of the answer.

Look at your life. Think about important decisions you have made, behaviors you exhibit, and the relationships you have—both good and not so good. Recall those who have impacted your values—parents, relatives, family, friends, teachers, bosses, mentors, religious leaders, and role models. Bring to mind the environments you experience—family, school, work, neighborhood, and the like. Make some notes as to how all this has shaped your values.

It is helpful to think about values from an ethic and a merit viewpoint. *Ethic* values are clear because they have a connotation of right or wrong. To be honest or have integrity means to tell the truth and not cheat. To have trust means to consistently keep your word. To be legal is to know and not break the law. Loyalty or fidelity is to be faithful to a vow or commitment. To be responsible is to take charge, execute, and be accountable for your actions, duties, and obligations. They are all easy to state but not so easy to consistently apply. *Merit* values, on the other hand, do not have a connotation of right and wrong. Rather, you determine where you want your value to be on a continuum. For example: the value of work from fairly easy to hard; self-improvement from "I'll just get by" to high achievement; physical health from "who cares?" to perfection; service to others from unimportant to the highest priority; total dependence to full independence; conservative to liberal; self-image from low esteem to high self-respect and pride; level of achievement from low and failing to high and excellent. You have choices for where you want your value to be on any merit continuum.

In his book *The Nature of Human Values*, Milton Rokeach provides another helpful way to classify them. He defines thirty-six operationally based concepts that are divided into two types of values: instrumental and terminal. Instrumental values are described as a means to an end and include such concepts as honesty, freedom, cleanliness, and responsibility. Terminal values are the "ends actually sought," including salvation, peace of mind, an exciting life, or a world at peace.

On the chart that follows, make a list of the *main* values you hold that guide the significant decisions you make, determine the behavior you exhibit, and choose your relationships with others. For which of those values would you like to improve the intent or clarity of the statement? For which of those values would you like to improve the consistency of application?

Important Values That Guide My Life	Satisfied with "My Standard of Excellence" for this Value		Satisfied with Consistent Application of this Value	
	Yes	No	Yes	No

You will have an opportunity to spend some time on this chart later in the book.

Morris Massey, renowned author and speaker, has written a fascinating book titled *The People Puzzle*. It deals with how folks with differing value systems, because of age group, race, or culture, can relate positively and work and enjoy life together. He provides an interesting chronological analysis of how one's values develop:

> From age 2 to 6, parents, deliberately or unaware, teach their children how to behave, think, feel and perceive. That early foundation for a value system is acted out by most without ever really questioning its validity. From 7 to 10 a child shifts into intense modeling—relating to family, friends, and "external heroes" around him. Somewhat blind acceptance gives way to selectivity. Group membership begins to exert its influence. People of like interests, behavior, and developing value systems associate intensely with one another. During the teen years young people engage in experimentation, verification and validation of a basic life plan—a dominant value direction. From 17 to 22, actual

transition and entry into the adult world is completed. The value system programmed during childhood and adolescence locks in, and is then tested against the reality of the world. College students seem particularly prone to do a lot of experimentation. Even though still under their parents' umbrella, some students try out lifestyles, living arrangements, political philosophies, and modes of behavior that may on the surface be in direct conflict with values programmed during their early development. At the end of that transition—age 22 plus—most young adults seem to revert back to their original programmed values. Then, when the financial umbilical cord to the family is cut, value systems will only change when challenged by significant emotional events. [2]

I would add that a value system can also be challenged for change by significant technological breakthroughs or major shifts in societal lifestyle.

What values one lives by and their relative importance is influenced and will vary depending on

- gender or ethnic or religious background;
- age group—teen, young adult, midlife, senior;
- economic status—wealthy, poor, or in between; and
- quality of life—very positive and satisfying, very negative and troubled, or somewhere in between.

Regardless of where you stand, you have listed the values important to you and which need improving and more consistent application. America's future as a country to live in, love, honor, and respect depends on each person improving his or her value system and its application in two ways. First, we must look at how our values impact our decision making, behavior, and relationships in all we do. We will cover that in chapter 3. Second, and equally or more important, we must look at how to share the application of those positive values more broadly across society where there is need—in the home, community, political arena, educational environment, religious sector, and the work place. That will be discussed in chapter 4.

We are all busy. School, work, raising a family, supporting the community, and the like are all hard and time consuming. A dedicated few can do all this and still find time to extend their positive ethical standards across society in many ways. For the active young and those in the midst of busy work and family lives, I ask you to consider only a realistic allocation of time to extend your values to those in need. For those who are "retired," or rather living life with more time and activity choices, I ask that your values' "give-back" time be greater. If we each give back to society as we are able, we can hold or turn America's values and resulting outcomes around. There will be many examples given for how to take stock of your values and guide you in how to share with those in need. If you join me in this "Renew American Values" crusade, we can save America's promise. Your rewards in terms of pride, self-respect, admiration, and the feelings of a truly meaningful life will far outweigh your time and effort.

Having positive values and beliefs makes life pleasant and worthwhile, but it does not make life easy! This world has many temptations—peer pressures, desires for more, ego gratification, overindulgence, false promises, and many more. Often those initially show up as minor, low-consequence, and one-instance diversions. We all know that enjoying one drug experiment, succeeding with one small lie, or benefiting from breaking one trust can begin the path to permanent value habits with serious long-term consequences. Just keeping and applying good virtues, so as not succumb to those temptations, takes consistent discipline, perseverance, and tough mental effort. To seek improvement in one's values and to broaden their application requires even greater dedication and passion.

Those of you who are now "giving back" and sharing your values in relationships and activities with others will have the easiest time fulfilling the promise of chapters 3 and 4. You know that those who do the most always make time to do more. Those of you with sound and positive values who are basically just living and enjoying the good life know that pride and reward could be much enhanced if you shared those values and your lifestyle by helping those in need. Those of you with mixed values and no actions to help those in need will require solid effort to internalize the promise of chapters 3 and 4. But the rewards are worth that effort. For those of you whose values are a negative shambles resulting in a life built around survival with no real thought of others, I can only suggest you read chapters 3 and 4 and give them a shot, be it ever so difficult. The world is full of stories of those who have seen the light, turned the corner, and become proud and contributing citizens.

There is a parable that has relevance here. One evening, an old American Indian told his grandson about a battle that goes on inside people. The battle is between two "wolves." One is destructive. It is envy, jealousy, greed, arrogance, self-pity, resentment, lies, and superiority, and it is judgmental. The other is good. It is peace, love, hope, serenity, humility, kindness, benevolence, empathy, generosity, truth, and compassion. The grandson thought about that and then asked, "Which wolf wins?" The old Indian replied, "The one you feed."

If one feeds those values that are positive, helpful, and uplifting, it makes it easier not to fail and to share one's virtues and lifestyle with others. That brings with it greater feelings of satisfaction, helpfulness, reward, and pride as we move through life. That is good! If one feeds the negative and hurtful values, that makes it easier to fail and leaves one with little positive to share with others. That turns life in a negative and unsatisfying direction with little self-worth and pride. That is not so good! While the choice is yours, I hope you see only one choice.

I promise you two rewards. First, from a nationwide perspective, if enough American leaders motivate enough citizens to lend support, we will bring back and then sustain and enhance America as the greatest place in the world to live for future generations. Second, from a personal perspective, the pride and sense of satisfaction you will receive will be well beyond your greatest other accomplishments.

With the origin of values in place, we move to guidelines to help you evaluate, sharpen, and improve the values that shape your life.

Chapter 3

IMPROVING VALUES AND

THEIR APPLICATION

In chapter 1, we saw that too often many of us live in a "me-first" world where it seems anything is okay if it produces immediate gain or success, regardless of the longer-term consequences. To improve on that, we need first to accept and internalize the answer to this question: why are sound and uplifting values important? Actually, the answer is quite simple. Values are the primary guide for decision making and behavior that lead to quality, fulfillment, and enjoyment of life—physical, mental, and moral. Transferring that importance into action is not so easy!

For the young, that means the reward of education, good jobs, health, success in their quests for independence, and the ability to cope with the temptations and pressures that confront them. For those in early adulthood and midlife, that means the pride and satisfaction of honest and hard work well done, the joy of love, the responsibility and reward of family, and the social/community pleasure of good friends and neighbors with whom to share quality of life. For seniors, that means a wealth of memories of a productive, contributing, and love-filled life, the joy and pride of children and grandchildren well raised, and the chance to pursue and enjoy life's choices that time and security provide. The greatest reward for all of the above is the opportunity and time to give of their values, capabilities, and assets to others in need.

As you read further through chapters 3 and 4, you will find several examples taken from northeast Florida where we live. These have their parallels in any state, city, community, family, business, or income level across the United States. All of these examples are provided not to belabor the point but to illustrate the many ways to sharpen values and broaden their application to improve your quality of life and that of others.

The book *It's How You Play the Game* by Brian Kilmeade helps answer the question of why values are important. It tells the stories of ninety-one individuals who hard wired sound values into their brains through youthful sports activities. For many, that helped make them outstanding amateur or professional athletes and persons. For well-known others, a career in sports was not their intent—rather just an important value-developing experience for their later successful lives. Some came from very troublesome environments. Some started with what turned out to be a false sense of self-worth. Some had great natural talent but little understanding of the hard work required to be their best. Some started thinking only of the glory of the ends and not the satisfaction of the process and the means. They all expressed that sports, with direct competition and outcomes, were the key to improving their ethics and results. And those improvements were embedded for life. For many, direct competition—in whatever the endeavor—is a good teacher to build sound virtues, regardless of the outcome.

Several of those quoted in the book commented on the support and contribution of their mothers and siblings to their successes in sports and in life. But the great majority commented on the support, teaching, and patience of their fathers. This is a great concern when it comes to values, as only 40 percent of children live in a home with a father.

Here are a few quotes from Kilmeade's book of what many said about their sports and later life experience.

> *I learned the ethic of hard work which I thrive on today. Knowing you have done your best far outweighs feelings of winning or losing.*
>
> —Dorothy Hamill, Olympic gold medal skater

> *Most of you are here because you have talent. But if you got here only on your talent, this may be your last game. What will take you to the top is attitude, loyalty, and integrity.*
>
> —Bill Yoast, high school coach from the film *Remember the Titans*

> *If you are willing to fail, you'll put yourself in situations to excel.*
>
> —Arthur Blank, founder, Home Depot

> *I hope people reading this will think more about honesty and integrity than championships. I was, and still to this day, am about the effort to succeed, not about the result.*
>
> —Arnold Palmer, professional golfer

> *No matter how good and big you think you are, there is always someone better and stronger.*
>
> President Abraham Lincoln (also a boxer)

The only discipline that lasts is self-discipline.

—Bum Phillips, NFL coach

Ability may get you to the top, but it takes character to stay there.

John Wooden, UCLA basketball coach

The important thing in the Olympic games is not to win, but to take part. The important thing in life is not the triumph, but the struggle.

—Baron Pierre De Coubertin, founder, modern Olympic Games

The trouble with most athletes is they take themselves seriously and their sport lightly.

—Mike Newlin, NBA player [1]

As I read these stories, I am reminded of my very best friend, Stan Sawczuk (now deceased). Stan grew up in the Polish section of Chicago where there were family values, but going off to college was not expected. He was a top athlete in high school and received a football scholarship to Purdue University. After graduation, he advanced in his career, becoming a senior executive at Merck. Stan had one of highest sets of values of anyone I have ever known. He always said, "If it hadn't been for sports, I never would have gone to college."

Improving Family Values

I am convinced that the foremost way to enhance and turn the decline in America's values around lies within the family. As we have seen previously, that is where our children's values are first developed and built into their brains and life. The family is the glue that holds society together in its practice of developing and applying sound principles with satisfying results.

John Rosemond, family psychologist, gives us some interesting insight when it comes to parenting.

Like most post-1960s parenting philosophy, "get involved with your children" is accepted not because of good sense or has proven to be advantageous (because it hasn't), but because it has a warm feel to it. There is a fine line between being involved and being supportive. Not so long ago in America, responsible parents kept track of but were not involved with their children. They knew where they were, what they were doing, and the friends in their children's lives, but they maintained a respectful distance, having their children learn their lessons by trial and error. When a child failed to act responsibly, his parents got involved with the consequence of less freedom. It did not take many such episodes for the child to get the point. Parenting requires leadership. This requires a boundary between the leader and the led, the permeability of which is controlled by the former. "Get involved with your children" puts the relationship before leadership, the cart before the horse. It often results in the distinction between parents and children being blurred, turning them into quasi-peers, thus making it difficult for the children to accept the parents' authority. High involvement transitions all too easily into micromanagement, in which case the child quickly learns that if he drops a proverbial "ball," his parents will not just pick it up, but probably also clean it up. Parents work harder and harder to make the child, who is working hardly at all, successful. Parents end up preventing most of the error in the child's trial-and-error process. The result is the child fails to learn important life lessons for life. [2]

Food for thought!

Shaunti Feldhahn adds the following in an editorial commentary:

Not only is it dangerous to be your kid's friend instead of their parent, I was stunned in my own research to learn that it isn't even what kids want—three out of four teenagers secretly wanted their parents to set and enforce real rules, instead of letting them do whatever they want. (3)

The key word in Feldhahn's comment is "instead." As long as parent and child understand parental responsibility and child accountability in situations where they are not peers, being friends in situations where they can be peers also develops sound values. Of course, how rules are applied and the relationships between parent and child change as families mature, sound values develop, and independence increases.

Dennis Todd, a school psychologist, also makes some telling points on the importance of ethics and parenting.

Child development experts find motivation, behavior, and achievement to be primarily the products of character and values, regardless of ethnic background, social status, or family income. Researchers now readily acknowledge that parental values are the most reliable predictors of child preferences in developing their relationships, religious practices, beliefs, work ethic, learning, and behavior. Silently enduring the massive assault on traditional values in the name of enlightened progressiveness is foolish and self-destructive. The price for not boldly advocating for responsible moral lifestyles will be costly for generations to come and eventually deadly for society. (4)

Dr. Frederick Porcase Jr. from Jacksonville—a family physician for thirty-three years—answers the question this way:

As a family physician, I have been practicing in Jacksonville for over 33 years. My practice has always touched the lives of patients across all socioeconomic classes, from millionaires to those with nothing. I can't begin to tell you how many teachers I have treated for anxiety and depression for classroom-related stress. I have lost count of all the good, dedicated ones who have simply quit out of frustration with the system. Now, parents think their child is right and the teacher is wrong. The 'political correctness' that has gained traction over many years has taken much of this discipline away. The War on Drugs is a joke! I have had so many young kids test positive you wouldn't believe it. Right and wrong have become indistinct. We need to return to some of the principles of the past or continue to suffer the consequences. [5]

Here is another rather extreme interpretation of parental responsibility. It was printed in the Scottsbluff, Nebraska, *Star-Herald* on November 13, 2008. I am sure some parents would consider this father an insensitive throwback to Neanderthal.

Two brothers, ages 12 and 15, were standing in the winter cold in front of the Dollar General Store holding signs that said: "My name is—I was caught shoplifting at Dollar General . . ." The father said that hopefully this will teach them that they need to make the right choices and that theft is not one of them. The best ending to the story was provided by the fifteen-year-old who said, "We will not do this again. We got in big trouble." They may not realize it now, but their parents taking this action in 2008 has greatly increased their chances of having productive and responsible lives. [6]

Obviously, parents have to decide the proper reward for a specific positive behavior and the proper penalty for a specific negative behavior. Either should be designed to encourage the positive and eliminate the negative and thus impact the value structure of the child in the right way. These decisions are better reached when the parents understand and follow "interested" versus "involved" relationships with their children.

Children and Media

Appropriate parenting also includes applying sound ethics with your children and the media they watch.

Eighty percent of 173 research studies over 28 years agree that heavy media exposure increases the harm of obesity, smoking, sex, drug and alcohol use, attention problems, and poor grades. The average child spends nearly 45 hours a week immersed in media, almost three times the amount of time they spend with their parents according to the report. In the past families often watched TV together and parents could easily change the channel to voice disapproval. Today's technology often isolates children who may tune out their families to concentrate on a cell phone screen only they can see. "The study provides overwhelming evidence of the importance of limiting children's use of media and teaching them to critically evaluate the ever-growing volume of text, images, and sounds with which they are bombarded," says co-author Ezekial Emanuel of The National Institutes of Health. [7]

Anita Chandra, a RAND Corporation behavioral scientist, reports the following on a new study—the first to link teens' TV viewing habits with sexual dialog and teen pregnancy:

> Groundbreaking research suggests that pregnancy rates are much higher among teens who watch a lot of TV with sexual dialog and behavior than among those who have tamer viewing tastes. Teens who watched the raciest shows were twice as likely to become pregnant over the next three years as those who watched fewer such programs. Psychologist David Walsh, President of the National Institute on Media and the Family, cited data suggesting only about 19% of American teens say they can talk openly with a trusted adult about sex. For a kid who no one's talking to about sex, and then he (she) watches sitcoms on TV where sex is presented

as this is what the cool people do, the outcome is obvious, Walsh said. [8]

Cell phones, blogs, iPods, social network sites, and the like—as well as electronic toys—present parents and their children with both opportunities and threats for value development leading to positive or negative outcomes. Reed Karaim quotes several experts on electronic media in the following excerpts.

Jane Healy, an educational psychologist:

> ... believes they're actually wiring kids' brains differently than in past generations. Many of the most popular and exciting video games engage and build the basic 'fight-or-flee' part of the brain rather than the centers of higher reasoning. If you watch kids on a computer, most of them are just hitting keys or moving the mouse as fast as they can. The rapid-fire pace of most electronic media is different from the sustained thought necessary for in depth reasoning, Healy says. She is convinced that pace can be tied to the dramatic increase in the diagnosis of attention-deficit disorder among today's children.

Gloria DeGaetano, an educator comments:

> There is an important theory in early child education called 'the theory of loose parts,' which means that children need to manipulate things in a three-dimensional environment to grow their brain. These video games and electronic toys are replacing the loose parts that kids need, and it is not the same

Author Lisa Guernsey says:

> For electronic toys and games, the best are those that allow a child the freest range of expression. The worst are those that

require a child to follow only narrow, preset patterns which not only stifle creativity, but also is frustrating to kids. [9]

New "texting" technology allows us to make visible and send almost anything to anyone without personal contact. The young love it, as it allows them to easily and frequently communicate and share with all their friends at once what they are doing, what they plan to do, what they are thinking about, and things that are going on. It allows them to organize activities, provide opinions on what they like and dislike, share good things that happen and not so good things to stay away from, and whatever else might be on their minds. It will become a powerful communication tool for any organization to quickly involve the appropriate people for information and opinions about a problem or decision at hand. It has tremendous potential as a marketing tool for both input and output. Think of its application in any major emergency or catastrophe.

But it has a downside—what you send is there forever in Internet space.

"Studies show that one in five teens has electronically transmitted explicit photos of themselves, and one-third say they have received such photos. It's a 21st century update of 'I'll show you mine' with one critical difference: lewd photos can be passed on and live forever on the Internet. But in many states, teens caught doing the same thing can risk felony charges, jail time and being branded sexual offenders." It is appropriate that these laws that now apply to this situation are being discussed for change from pornography to stupidity with the proper resulting penalties. [10]

This technology can create new types of value risks. Stephen Young, executive director of the ethics-focused Caux Round Table says the following:

"Contemporary American culture is drifting toward shallowness, selfishness and pettiness and away from respect for ourselves and, therefore, a corresponding respect for others." He blames a society that increasingly relies on faceless communication—e-mails, text messages, cell phones—and the resulting omnipotence that brings. "I think we all feel that we're more able to exploit our power, take advantage of others, when they're anonymous and there are no consequences. It's that corrupting sense of power that comes when we lose a sense of responsibility and accountability." [11]

Technology can't be blamed for the problem, and curtailing new technology is not the answer. The answer is using new technology with principles and accountability. Kids had cameras before, but I don't recall a lot of publicity about the circulation of nude photos. Ethical standards about right and wrong, decency, privacy, and shame at being caught were in place. While protective monitoring software can help, that will not solve the problem. Parents are responsible. For example, rules for the use of cell phones and methods to check that use should be agreed on at time of purchase and then followed. Ethics like honesty and trust must be a part of this process.

There is good news. Lisa Tripp of Florida State University reports the following from detailed research of the Digital Youth Project:

There are many reasons for adults to embrace and even facilitate digital media . . . most young people almost always associate with those they already know from their offline lives. A smaller number use online to find information not available at school or in the community, and to connect with people who share specialized interests like creative writing. Youth respect one another's (their peer's) authority online and are often motivated to learn more from each other than adults. Tripp says she would like to see adults gain more technical skill so they can be more involved in what their children are doing. [12]

James Mehring quotes Susan Thomas, author of *Buy, Buy Baby*, in a *Business Week* article:

". . . consumerism trumps learning as companies try to infiltrate nearly every aspect of a child's life." But the major focus is on the newborn to age 3 bracket. "Companies are capitalizing on widespread anxiety that children must be stimulated to learn from Day One and the belief, especially among gen X parents, that TV is a legitimate educational tool for babies. . . . there is little proof that these Digital Age offerings do a better job than wooden blocks at making babies smarter. How do parents counter this multimedia marketing blitz? For one thing, they must quash the idea that kids need stimulation at all times. Instead, parents should spend time doing 'nothing,' allowing 'adults and their young children to have periods of unstructured time when they can see what just unfolds.'" [13]

I propose the conclusion here is for parents and children to agree on acceptable-usage ground rules for these new electronic media when acquired. Then parents need to learn enough about them, independently and through their kids, so they can discuss and be involved in the constructive learning and fun they can provide. For example, it is okay for children beyond the age of reason (seven or so) to pick what they want to watch on TV with parental approval. But there should be a mix to include things the parents pick that will be interesting and life expanding for their children.

Talk with your children about these things long before they are teens. Explain the potential outcomes to the lives of those who overindulge and are not careful about their media involvement. Agree on limits of acceptable TV—perhaps two hours a day. Let them help you learn about new media technology and positive and not-so-positive uses. Don't rely on ratings for video games. Play some yourself and with your children. Think about not allowing children to have computers, TV, or other media in their bedrooms. Keep communications open—let them know you are there to discuss any concerns or issues they might have over the intent and how to respond to media messages they receive. Set the example!

Setting that example requires parents to think about these things. "Walk the talk" and examine your behavior as a role model. Keep up on technology, and know your children's friends and activities, or you may be duped—or at least seen as uninterested—and your guidance not followed. It is more effective to help your children learn good values and habits by understanding their lives and participating in "peer" activities than by just controlling their potential bad habits by limiting TV time.

Family Values and Health

The family must be concerned with ethical standards that apply to health. Obesity is a growing American concern for both children and adults. Here are some specific thoughts on childhood obesity (many are just as valuable for overweight adults):

> The obesity rate for teens has tripled over the past 25 years, and with this increase in average weight, type 2 diabetes, once unknown in young people, is now diagnosed in 45% of all new cases of obesity involving children or teens. For many parents with an obese child the things they have tried haven't worked. Dr. Kathy McCoy, author of *The Teenage Body Book,* explains how you can help your teen lose weight and feel better.

- Put the emphasis on good health, not weight, and make it a goal for the whole family. Teens hate being singled out and criticized.
- An approach to this from a "YOU need to lose weight" will guarantee a battle of the wills. Instead, ask for your teen's help in developing an action plan to promote better family eating and exercise habits.
- Have real family meals at least once a day and encourage your teen to eat what the family eats. Frantic family schedules have equaled fast food or prepared food dinners and expanding waist lines. With real home-cooked meals,

you can better control calories, fats, sugars, sodium and other nutritional issues.

- Look at and discuss all of your less-than-ideal eating behaviors. Pay attention to the difference between physical and emotional hunger. Discuss all of this with your family and come up with ways to comfort or reward yourselves that have nothing to do with food.
- Make it convenient for everyone in the family to eat breakfast.
- Schedule exercise into your family routine; exercise is good for everyone. Trying to motivate an overweight teen to go to the gym can be frustrating and non-productive.
- There are no weight loss miracles. The weight did not come on overnight and can't be lost—for good—overnight. The goals should be health improvement with a slow, steady weight loss of no more than two pounds a week.
- Make a vow—together—to enjoy a full and healthy life now. Don't wait until the weight is gone. Good nutrition, regular exercise, and the feeling that "we're all in this together" can make a positive difference for everyone in your family. [14]

In addition, the federal surgeon general suggests the following:

- Let your child know he or she is loved and appreciated whatever his or her weight.
- Focus on your child's health and positive qualities, not your child's weight.
- Be a good role model for your child.
- Provide a safe environment for your children and their friends to play actively; encourage swimming, biking, skating, ball sports and other fun activities. [15]

It is only through these guides that ethical standards about pride, moderation, and self-control are permanently wired to guide future health and weight decisions for our youth.

Obesity is not just a youth problem. Trust for America's Health and the Robert Wood Johnson Foundation report the following:

"In 1995, no state had an obesity rate above 20 percent. The state with the lowest obesity rate now—Colorado, with 19.8% of adults considered obese—would have had the highest rate in 1995." The ten most obese states scored 34.4 to 30.5 percent and the ten least 24.3 to 19.8 percent. "About a third of the adults who did not graduate from high school are obese; about a fifth of those who graduated from college are considered obese." [16]

It is time parents, students, educators, the government, and businesses brought sound virtues back into decisions about what we eat and the amount we exercise—portions are too large, too many fast foods and packaged foods are unhealthy, school lunch choices can be unhealthy, and reasonable exercise for too many has bitten the dust.

Alcohol remains the young's number-one drug of choice and is the most problematic drug in our society. Too many parents find it their number-one choice of drugs and have accepted underage drinking as a "rite of passage." Sadly, that indifference is limiting potential and destroying lives every day.

"Instead of keeping their kids locked out of the liquor cabinet, parents turn out to be the primary suppliers of alcohol to young adolescents, according to a new study from the Universities of Florida and Minnesota. By the time adolescents reach fourteen, 33 percent report having a drink within the past year, and the largest percentage of these teens said they got their last drink from an adult over 21." Kelly Kumro, an associate professor at the University of Florida and senior author concludes: "For parents, of course, the important message is for them to understand that it is risky to provide alcohol for their children. It increases the risk of teen drinking, which in turn increases a young person's risk for alcohol-related problems all the way into adulthood." [17]

This would not be a bad subject for family discussion and for example setting.

New research from the University of Oslo reports telling conclusions from four collective, if obvious, bad habits.

> Those in one group smoked tobacco, drank (more than three alcoholic beverages a day for men; two in the case of women), exercised less than two hours a week, and ate few fruits and vegetables. Twenty-nine percent of that group died within 20 years, often as a result of heart disease or cancer. Only 8 percent of those with healthier habits died during those years. [18]

So, if you enjoy life and want to live it fully, take heed!

Ultimately, the consistent application of sound and uplifting ethical standards leads to lives filled with satisfaction and reward for things well done—the fulfillment from a productive work career, the love and respect of family, the pride for serving one's community and country, the joy of helping others in need, and the peace of a good night's sleep.

Values and Change

I am not writing this book to suggest we return to "the good old days." That has always been said to the younger generation as the older watched the world around them. As my father always said, "We are going to hell in a hand basket." There are no good old days, but it can be helpful to look back. It helps to first look back to find outcomes that were consistently positive in the past but now are not and the sound values that drove them, what happened to those values, and how to bring them back to regain positive outcomes. Secondly, it helps to look back to find outcomes that were not acceptable in the past and are not acceptable now, the values that drove them, and how to improve them and their application to improve those outcomes. Thirdly, it helps to look back on past ways of living and finding what didn't work out very well, what values failed us, and how to do a better job of applying sound and relevant values to assure success in ever-changing new future ways of life.

Today, successfully adapting to more frequent change is difficult. Life in any past span of years certainly did not have the benefits of the current world, but things seemed more in place and understood. For example, when our generation grew up:

- the choices we could make were more limited and fixed;
- most people had the benefit of consistent lifestyles by staying where they were;
- differences between the good and bad guys were understood and stayed that way;
- soldiers wore uniforms;
- penalties for deviations from what was expected were known and applied;
- marriage was the accepted family lifestyle, and divorce was rare;
- most children had parents, and family was more sacred;
- dads went to work, and moms stayed home;
- children had more self-creative time and space to grow up;
- life's experience opened up at more appropriate stages when it could be understood and appreciated;
- the rate of change was slower, with more time to enjoy what was current;
- children went to school and church;
- the local community was where life existed; and
- kissing a girl was a thrill.

I am sure each generation can paint its nostalgia when life was more stable. But you can't go back!

Change continues to accelerate.

For example, it took 71 years for the telephone to reach 50% of our homes while it took only 7 years for DVD players. [19]

As another example, since the invention of the integrated circuit in 1958, the number of transistors that can be placed inexpensively on an integrated circuit has doubled every two years.

Change is constant across society, including:

- new technology and outputs from current technology;
- new social approaches to family structure and lifestyle;
- new government policies and interventions;
- judges making law versus interpreting law; and
- new interpretations of traditional ethical and moral values.

Those changes create exciting opportunities to modify and improve our lives and the lives of those around us. But we must be careful! Sometimes, the technology itself can cause unconscious temptations to an otherwise sound principle, such as financial prudence. Take the credit card. Researchers have found that users buy more products and services with plastic than they did with cash or check. That is true whether you pay up every month or carry debt. Greg Davies at Britain's Warwick University, who researched this, says:

Credit cards reduce the pain of payment because of the following: payment is put off and you don't do the same mental accounting as with cash; buying several items at one time on a single credit transaction gives no clear signal that we may have overspent on any one item; payment by cash imprints on the brain that you are letting go of some cash. Try paying cash for a month and compare it to the previous credit card month. [20]

Change and Right and Wrong

As far as legality and values and change, Ted Schroder, pastor at our Amelia Plantation Chapel, makes this point from a Christian perspective:

> Legal permissiveness on a host of privacy issues does not constitute validation from a biblical moral perception. Just because someone is allowed by law to do something, or get away with something, does not mean it is sanctioned for the Christian disciple. Jesus made it quite clear that the moral commandments are not dependent on public opinion. The Ten Commandments are the same today, and are as valuable today for our worship and our relationships, as they ever have been. They provide us with the direction we need to fulfill our destiny, and to develop our character. [21]

This is worthy of thought whether you are a Christian or not.

Duke University's Fuqua School of Business scandal suggests the possibility that we may have new interpretations of cheating.

10% of the 2008 MBA class . . . which averaged 29 years old with 6 years corporate experience . . . had been caught cheating on a take-home final exam. This was at a time when their bosses were touting the new world of Linux open source where one's ability to aggregate others' intellectual property was seen as a competitive advantage. Working together on a take-home exam is not academic fraud; its post-modern learning and text messaging exam answers or downloading essays onto iPods is simply a wise use of technology. "We are told it's all about teamwork and shared information. But then we are graded and ranked as individuals. We assess everybody as single entities. But then we plop them into an interdependent world and tell them their success hinges on creative collaboration." [22]

We will have to find new ways to test and assess educational progress, and that may change historical ideas about cheating. But there will still be appropriate rules about honesty. If it was known that the take-home final test was to be completed individually, then doing it collectively was cheating.

Our outstanding universities with classic MBA programs are modifying those programs to put more focus on the notion of sound codes of ethics as critical to an organization's long-term strategic and operational decisions and survival. As the first sentence in the next quote suggests, this will not be easy. In my judgment, the point made is long overdue. Too often, ethics and values have been treated as the "soft stuff" when compared with subjects like finance, economics, computer science, and the like.

Harvard Business School, for example, is changing its curriculum, but whether it can reform business school culture remains to be seen. It would significantly revamp its M.B.A. program, adding new required courses on ethics and teamwork. The changes are also part of an effort to diffuse what many see as a money-hungry culture that prevails at elite business schools—a culture some say helped create the recent crisis on Wall Street. "The public lost confidence in business, and some of our graduates seem to be responsible for that," says Nitin Nohria, who was appointed dean of the school in July 2010. There is a growing sense that students don't care what goes on in the classroom, only about the connections they are developing among themselves. [23]

It is a start! In my opinion, those leading this MBA change in our business schools need to make this an extensive effort. They should involve and take input and suggestions from (1) their graduates who have ethical and successful track records, (2) top industry leaders who believe and practice that basic beliefs and teamwork are the key to long-term business success, and (3) leaders and practitioners in consulting, financial service, and Wall Street who have demonstrated consistent application of sound ethical standards in their decisions and investments. That input should create a new curriculum that will work. Then it must be given the same credibility and importance as programs that are currently more widely accepted. As a final suggestion, it also should require a honing of the candidate selection process to seek those who are successful long term because they have a sound code of ethics and have demonstrated they use it. On the other side, it is time to be more selective and consider not accepting candidates who might seem successful but show little respect for ethical standards.

New lifestyles can be value traps. Ted Schroder has written a book titled *Solid Love*. He makes the comparison between "solid love" and "liquid love." He quotes Zygmunt Bauman from his book *Liquid Love*:

Post-modern relationships are seen as lacking commitment. Relationships are fluid, untrustworthy, and unlikely to last. The meaning of the word love has been devalued. Sexually it describes a passing experience rather than an enduring affection. Love is seen as a skill, a commodity in a consumer culture that can be acquired at little cost to the customer. Like availability of credit, casual love takes the "waiting out of wanting." Partnerships are not expected to last a lifetime. A relationship is an investment, and, like a stock, you hold it as long as it promises to rise in value, and sell it when it begins to falter. You are at the mercy of constant evaluation. When the tide of "love" runs out, there is a feeling of being used, being depleted, rejected, of having failed to please. This is also true for serial marriage—the marriages that do not last but end in divorce. Many times such a marriage is doomed because one of the partners is not prepared to grow in solid love for the other. Instead of the relationship being affirming and life-giving, it is characterized by hurt and abuse.

Pastor Schroder responds with the following:

Solid love is meant to endure all vicissitudes: love never ends. It requires concentration, thought, effort, willpower, motivation, and application. Learning to love is the task of a lifetime. It is the challenge to grow into maturity. It is the journey to wholeness. It is the struggle of unselfishness over self-centeredness. Soren Kierkegaard expressed the character of love in many of his writings: "What is it that makes a person great, admired by creation, well pleasing in the eyes of God? What is it that perseveres when everything falls away, that comforts when all comfort fails, that is never changed even though everything is changed—it is love." [24]

So, those who foster new forms of living and relating, and all of us who live with them, must be careful to consider the potential implications on our values. If we make and implement those new lifestyle changes to improve and strengthen values that lead to better long-term lives, then we all gain, our society is preserved, and those values stay firmly planted in our brains. If we make and apply those lifestyle changes mainly for immediate gratification, that can mean rationalizing or forsaking our values and discounting longer-term consequences. That can start the process leading to very unsatisfying long-term lives. We each have those choices. Hopefully this book will give you the reasons and the process to choose the right one for you.

Values and Life

Values develop from the environment and the way a person lives life at work, at home, in the community, at school, through religion, and so on. We are influenced by parents, siblings, relatives, family, friends, teachers, leaders, role models, mentors, and the like. I suppose we could debate forever whether life's experiences primarily determine our values or whether our values primarily determine life's experiences. In our formative, growing-up years, this is an iterative process between the two. In very early childhood, beliefs are primarily influenced by the home environment and those in it who train and set the example. Then they are gradually firmed in more positive or negative directions by testing and experiences outside the home and discussed, critiqued, and further shaped in the home. This leads to gradual independence where learned ethical and moral principles increasingly influence decisions, behavior, and relationships. I believe that by the time one reaches the high school graduation age, most of the virtues that will guide the rest of life are fairly hard wired in one's brain.

That is certainly true, as they influence decisions, behavior, and relationships throughout the ups and downs along our "normal," day-by-day stream of life. With caution, they can be tweaked or reinterpreted to enter into any new and beneficial situation. Without that caution, what appeared as beneficial could, in reality, be negative with corresponding consequences. Perhaps the best way to take advantage of sound, implanted values in day-by-day life is to structure the environment or situation to take better advantage of them. For example, good managers have learned that it is very difficult to change mature adult behavior with its strengths and weaknesses. So, they find what people are good at and give them more and what they are not good at and give them less. The right mix of "goods" and "not so goods" among the team makes it all productive. If a person is not good enough to be a successful team member, managers replace that person. It may seem like a hard-nosed tactic, but that's business life in reality.

Beyond modest situational changes, only a significant emotional event, a major new opportunity, or a technological innovation can cause us to consider and potentially adapt our ethical standards. A new value direction can either lead to positive or negative outcomes. If careful thought suggests that a new direction can be positive and will improve quality of life and/or society, go for it. If a proposed new direction seems risky beyond its benefits, beware. Think of the potential long-term consequences to your quality of life and society and then act accordingly.

Given these realities as far as *change* and *life*, how do we explore improving those values that guide our lives and seek more consistent application? While it is a challenge to classify people by their ethical standards and life, it is helpful to do this as a starting point. I admit at the outset that this is an arbitrary segmentation of a values-lifestyle-outcome continuum. Folks with generally good values sometimes go wrong, and folks with generally poor values sometimes do well. I needed some way to help one locate where he or she lives, makes choices, behaves, and relates to others along this continuum. That provides a starting point from which to improve.

I decided on a three-fold classification of people based on the environment in which their values developed, what that could mean for dealing with life's temptations, and where that might lead in the longer term. They are *fortunate, mixed,* and *unfortunate.* Having positive values and beliefs makes life pleasant and worthwhile, but it does not make life easy. This world has many temptations—peer pressures, desires for more, ego gratification, overindulgence, false promises, and immediate gain. Often, those initially show up as minor, low-consequence, and one-instance diversions. But we know that enjoying one cigarette or drug experiment, succeeding with one little lie, or benefiting from breaking one trust can lead to serious long-term consequences. Just keeping and applying good virtues, so as not to succumb to those temptations, takes consistent discipline, perseverance, and tough mental effort. To seek improvement in one's principles and broaden their use requires even greater dedication and passion. It doesn't take much discipline to enjoy the short-term gains for succumbing to temptation and putting off the long-term consequences. By the same token, it is easier to apply good values to the enjoyment of life and ignore others with needs—"That is not my responsibility—let the government, educational system, business, church, community, and nonprofit charities handle those needs."

Fortunate

This includes those who have been raised with good values and loving parents, with reasonable standards of living, among solid friends, in generally safe communities, and where high expectations like education were the rule. In other words, they had most everything positive going for them in the development of their values, including knowledge of how to handle temptations most of the time and a high probability for excellent and fulfilled lives. Typically, in their youth, they didn't have to face or learn to avoid really serious challenges to their ethical and moral systems. Then, as they traveled into adult life, their main issues revolved around not being very street smart as they were faced with new and different environments and conditions. They brought to that the advantage of good values instilled in their brains and experience from the benefits in their actions. When tempted in a new situation, that put a helpful roadblock in the way. Those in the *fortunate* position have lots going for them to succeed and excel in life no matter the routes they choose.

Mixed

This includes those who grew up in an environment with both positive and negative conditions and mentors around them as their values developed. That made it more difficult to successfully cope with life's temptations. For them, that meant both good and not-so-good beliefs were instilled with appropriate outcomes. Their quality of life had ups and downs. One main issue as their values developed was to seek situations and relationships that enhanced the hard wiring of their positive values. Another issue was finding new ways of dealing with or avoiding situations and relationships that would enhance their not-so-positive values. Or, they could just go either way depending on the situation and just let life take its course. I would wish them more in life than that. Those in the *mixed* position have to be a lot more thoughtful and careful of the routes they choose to succeed and have satisfying lives.

Unfortunate

This includes those who grew up with very little going for them. They faced poverty, dysfunctional families, abuse, poor schools, crime, drugs, no or few positive mentors and role models, and so on. They had little help in resisting the serious temptations they faced and the negative values instilled as a result. Their main value challenge in early life, if they decided to take it, was to seek help and try to find those few positive opportunities that existed in that environment and to try not to succumb to those that were negative. Then, in early adult life, some figured out how to escape their environment, find ways to make it better, or live better with it. For some, that happened because an organization or individual took a personal interest in helping them improve their quality of life. Many others just fell into and stayed "lost" with life and survival in that early negative environment. These folks have the toughest route to a successful quality of life, but with help, the drive to succeed, and perseverance, it can be done. They can learn from many others who have done just that.

While these classifications are arbitrary, try to locate yourself in or near one.

My granddaughter Sarah provides a good example to illustrate *fortunate*. She was raised by loving and value-driven parents in a middle-class home in a solid community. This positioned her with positive ethical standards and a good quality of life. While in high school on a Halloween "mischief night," she was at a girlfriend's house and needed a ride home. Some boys, who were friends, dropped by and offered to take her. On the way, they stopped by the house of a boy not in their group and spray-painted various places on his car. Sarah tried to convince them not to do it, but to no avail. The boy found out who did the spray painting and got in a fight with one of them at the school. They ended up in the principal's office along with the other boys involved. They all denied having done it. They urged Sarah to support them. After much thought, her values prevailed, and she told the truth. The boys who did it were all on the hockey team, and they were punished by suspension from several games. Those boys and their "girls," whom Sarah also counted as friends, ostracized her and made her school and social life very unpleasant. Some of her teachers penalized her for her action. Some of the boys' and girls' parents let her know how they felt. The boy whose car was painted was grateful.

Sarah wondered for a while if the consequences were worth the truth. But in the long run, she knew she learned what real friends were all about, and she realized the value path she might have started down if she had lied. No one ever said that applying ethical values would always be easy. What would you have done if you were Sarah?

The boys and girls who did this were basically good kids. They were tempted, did something wrong, and tried to deny it. Hopefully, they have realized what their actions did to the boy, to Sarah, and to their own sense of self-respect and integrity. That would make an interesting study.

If you grew up in the *fortunate* category, value risks you faced as you moved into early adult life were potentially new environments and relationships that you were not used to. Khalil Gibran says in his most famous book, *The Prophet*:

> You are good when you walk toward your goal firmly. You are not evil when you go thither limping. Even those who limp do not go backward. But, you who are strong and swift see that you do not limp among the lame, deeming kindness. [25]

Think carefully about new temptations, and apply your good code of ethics to your decisions and behavior. Don't get sucked in to be accepted. The other values risk you face is succumbing to small, seemingly one-time temptations that could have immediate benefits. If you falter once, don't make it a habit. And when that happens, keep your good values up front and always take time to think of longer-term risks or serious consequences succumbing to that temptation might produce.

How could one smart guy like former New York Governor Elliot Spitzer be so stupid? He ruined a career and life he spent decades building up. He left himself vulnerable to criminal punishment, humiliated himself and his family in the eyes of the world all for a few nights in the sack with a whore. The most obvious answer to his self-destructive act is that he let the immediate pleasure of his value temptation overwhelm any thoughts about the long-term risks and by rationalizing that he wouldn't be caught. [26]

And then there is the saga of Tiger Woods. As he implied in his first press conference, his unique prominence at the top of his world eventually caused him to think he was entitled to do what he did. That is a severe ethical drop from the role model of the very successful and happily married man he had presented. It will be interesting to see how long it will be, if ever, for his golfing prowess to return and how society will finally judge him.

The Tiger Woods story has shades of a former president, but the reactions and results were very different.

But there are many others like my granddaughter:

Grandmother Billie Watts of Murfreesboro, TN, found $97,000 stuffed into a purse at a Cracker Barrel restaurant and she could have made good use of that money as she lives on Social Security. But she did what came naturally to her and devised a plan to return the money to the rightful owner. She phoned the restaurant, said she had found "something" in the bathroom, and left her number. She was able to return the money belonging to a woman who had just sold her home and was on her way to Florida to start a new life with her son. Watts refused a $1,000 reward because the woman "told me she needed every penny she could to start over." It's an uplifting reminder that people do live by character—it's how you behave when no one is looking. [27]

Rex Kastner, a close friend and neighbor at our summer home in Minnesota, agreed he was a fitting example for the *mixed* category as he grew up. I am much older than he and knew him first as a teenager. His father died when he was young. His mother was a wonderful, caring, and community-minded Christian lady who loved him much, but, I am afraid, gave him too much uncontrolled latitude and time at too early an age. After high school graduation, he stayed with local friends who did not go off to college, and he began to do things that showed questionable values that were very different from those his mother embodied. Partying—and the alcohol and drugs and girls that went with it—became a norm. But, on the plus side, sometimes he was on the up-and-up—bright, outgoing, fun to be with, always willing to help, and dedicated to his mother. He was creative in coming up with and working at many well-intentioned but unrealistic schemes to build a business and make money.

So, he had a mixed bag with respect to values. Some were good with longer-term positive implications. Some were not so good, resulting in immediate gratification but beginning to plant those values in his brain. With no one to really provide council as to where he was headed and what to do about it, the bad outcomes began to outweigh the good ones. It was at this point that I got involved.

He and my youngest son, Jim, were summer friends enjoying lake activities like his wood-fired sauna. One day, they came home with a pickup truck full of split hardwood. In talking with them separately, their stories of how they acquired the wood did not quite match. Being the "bulldozer" my wife says I am, I confronted them about this together. They denied any wrongdoing. A bit later, they came back and admitted that they had stolen it from a farmer's field. We had a little talk about ethics and consequences, and they returned the wood.

For Jim, that was a value temptation and a lesson learned. Rex felt regret, but it really wasn't a lesson learned except for his respect for me. That began a mentoring which continued over the years.

He was a born salesman and always had jobs in that field. At home, he was a good and fun-loving son and neighbor. But he got into what turned out to be a very bad marriage, which added more questionable "friends" to his life. Bad habits increased, and drugs, alcohol, and police were involved. A difficult divorce followed.

I helped him see that the only road back to improving his life was to get out of that environment and away from his friends. He went away to college and graduated. He made new friends. He continued his career in sales and has risen to vice president of sales in his firm. He found and married a wonderful woman who is a positive "rock." He looked after his mother until her death. He is a good father to his daughter from his first marriage and a caring grandfather. His values and life are on the right track.

For some of you in—or close to—the *mixed* category, this may seem a fairly extreme negative-to-positive mixed values example. If so, any quest you might make for a more satisfying and rewarding future will be easier than his.

The risk you face in *mixed* is continuing to succumb to temptations. The immediate gain or benefit will reinforce more negative values to dominate your life. That often can lead to involvement in less desirable situations and less focus on the positives. Kevin Hart of Fernley, Nevada, did just that.

He was a two-star offensive lineman who gathered family, coaches, and classmates in the gym to announce his college choice. He said he had fielded offers from five Division 1 schools and had chosen California because Coach Jeff Tedford did most of the recruiting of him. But Tedford had never talked to Hart, nor had Oregon, Nevada, Washington or Oklahoma State. After numerous media blamed the incident on a recruiting con man, Hart admitted he made up the entire story: "When I realized that wasn't going to happen, I made up what I wanted to be reality." [28]

Sadly, at that point, that could have cost him any offer.

The key is, when you are tempted, seek help and guidance from every advisor, leader, friend, and mentor that supports the positive parts of your life. For every decision you plan to take, every behavior you plan to exhibit, and every relationship you plan to have, consider the long-term risks to your value system and your life versus any short-term pleasures or benefits.

The following life story dramatically and shockingly illustrates *unfortunate*. I tell it in some detail to show the majority who are not in *unfortunate* how easy it will be to improve their lives. And even more importantly, the collective impact we can have on preserving American culture and promise by sharing our values and lives with others. I also chose this story to convince those in or near *unfortunate* that their lives cannot be worse than this man's. If he could turn his life and values around and then help others in need, so can others. We can all agree that this is a most difficult challenge, but it can be done, and the rewards are great.

This story began with a phone call from my long-ago college roommate and close friend, Jim Moore. He was one of many I asked to help with this book. Jim had read an article in his local paper about the story of a man in prison. He was touched by the story, spoke with the writer, and decided to go to the prison to talk with this man. He met and counseled with him several times. The man, Jerry Louvier, served his time and was released. Jim summarized that over the phone and gave me Jerry's phone number and suggested I call him to see if he would give me his full story to use in this book. Jerry agreed and told me he was writing a small book about his life and would send me a copy. The book is titled *Why Me Lord?* It is not available in general publication. I have paraphrased his life in first person as he told it.

When I was seven, my mother left with three of my siblings. I do not know what I did to be left behind. My father worked all the time and spent most of the rest in bars, finding women for six marriages. Most of my stepmothers were mean and drunks. My first one was big and very mean. She and my father fought terrible fights until my dad and I left. I stayed with my grandmother, who I liked. I got in with a cousin and began stealing and selling stuff for money. My father went back to his wife. She finally left, locking me in a closet for two days where my dad found me.

Stepmother two worked at a liquor store and was drunk every night. I would end up at my grandmother's with my cousin. Whenever I got in juvenile detention, my uncle would bail me out, and my father would beat me. Stepmother three was a little better, but I smoked and drank and quit school in the sixth grade. Then my older brother came to live with us. He was mean and beat me all the time. Dad got tired of this and took off his belt and told me he would whip me if I didn't beat up my brother. Three fights and three whippings later, I finally won. My brother got whipped.

The last time my uncle bailed me out, he made a deal for me to join the army. In Vietnam, I learned the real truth of that war and saw so much of what shouldn't have happened. I saw so many Americans blown up or missing body parts that I developed a "get even" mind-set. I began to enjoy killing. You never trusted anybody—the Cong put hand grenades under their babies that would blow up when you picked them up. The smell of death was the worst—we removed our dead, but the Cong just left theirs to rot. There, I learned to smoke dope and use drugs.

Two days before I was to go home, a friend and I went to a village to get drunk. On the way back to camp, I shot some people as a form of revenge. That "friend" told me that I should plead guilty and would get off lightly with the military. I did that and got forty years of hard labor, lost my medals, and received a dishonorable discharge. They shipped me home in my shorts in a metal container.

I went to Leavenworth, and little did I know that there was something worse than Vietnam. After three days, I beat a prisoner half to death with a mop wringer because the guy said he was going to make me his girl. Getting drugs in prison was like going to the store. The guards were the main suppliers. I got in trouble a lot and was put into the "hole"—solitary confinement. Think of the worst thing you can, and that was the hole. Multiple guards would beat you if you caused them any trouble.

I transferred prisons and stabbed a guy for the same reason as before. You have to earn your respect to survive in there. When it was time for prisoner war, you prepared and picked the right spot and time—*Life* magazines under your shirt to stop a knife; Vaseline all over so you couldn't be held; a rolled-up towel between your legs. You would scream to gain a couple of seconds that could save your life.

Marion Maximum Security Prison opened and took in the worst in the system—including me. I kept getting into trouble. I had done the longest time on record for a military prisoner of war. When I finally hit bottom, I decided that good behavior was the only way to ever get out. I started getting time reductions and wrote letters to the press. The Vietnam Veterans Against the War began to help. I got transferred to the Terre Haute, Indiana Federal Prison. A CEO sat on my parole board and promised me a job if they would let me out.

I got out, got the job, and the CEO helped me make it for six months in a halfway house. But hatred was my survival, and I trusted no one. I lost the job, and no one would hire an ex-con. I had a probation officer who didn't care if I made it or not. I felt so alone I wanted to be back with my prison brothers—my only family.

Then I met Jeannie, and we had dinner—and that started our lives together. She went to my parole meetings. I met her family, and their values were good and clean. I slept on the couch until we were married. Jeannie went to church, but I still hated God and blamed him for my life. God was a sign of weakness in prison; no one would turn the other cheek. I continued to smoke dope and drink, but not in front of Jeannie.

I could not get a real job, so I went door-to-door asking people if they needed anything done. A friend got me a union job making five dollars an hour. Jeannie and I were married in a simple ceremony in her basement. We built a house, had a son, and life was looking up. Our house got flooded out several times, and I raised it up on stilts to solve the problem. Neighbors saw this, and soon, I was able to buy equipment and did this for a living.

Moving my values and life back up at this point came with small problems and successes. I took my crew out after some hard work, and we got drunk. When I got home in the morning, Jeannie and I argued, and I drove my fist through the wall. Jeannie took a baseball bat and knocked holes in the wall all the way down the hall. I fixed them and never did that again. Another time, at a bar listening to a friend's son's band—and in Jeannie's absence–-I smoked a joint. She returned, and I got caught. She asked for the car keys and left. It was midwinter, and my friends offered to take me home. I said, "No, she will come back for me." After an icy walk home, I quit smoking pot. One night at my birthday party, we were drinking. I always marked my bottle to know when to stop. The guys distracted me and kept refilling the bottle. I did not suspect and got drunk. My two sons carried me home, and I have not gotten drunk since.

I bought a house-raising machine, and with all the floods and work, I felt I became the best in the business. I joined a large firm, and we did big jobs like moving the Cape Hatteras lighthouse, the King of Prussia Inn in Pennsylvania, and a Newark air terminal. I gained national recognition, including a stop on *Good Morning America*.

But with all this improvement in my life, hatred kept eating my insides, and I took pills to stay out of trouble. Jeannie went to church to see her grandson in some function, and I went with her. But I did not want to change; feelings are troublesome for a gangster. Little did I know how soon I would realize what I had missed in my life. With Jeannie, I saw *The Passion of the Christ* and this was a life-changing experience for me. I wanted to do something to get rid of the hatred, but I did not think the church would take me. I told my story to the pastor and gave him my word, which is honorable, that I would try my best to change. To my surprise, the pastor opened his arms, and Jeannie and I asked God to come into our lives. We were baptized on April 25, 2004. I never had so many people wanting to shake my hand and say hello. I shook hands with a black man, and while my skin crawled, I now know that he and I were no different. While I worship, my high is greater than any I remember doing drugs. I took full advantage of the church's offerings. I was empty and wanted to be full. Jeannie and I went on mission trips. We found a church with no air conditioning and led fundraising to buy one. A family near us lost their home in a fire. I asked all the companies I worked with, along with the church, to help. We rebuilt the home and stocked it with furniture and food. That family began going to church with us and were baptized to give their lives to God. No money could buy what they gave back to me. I hire ex-cons for my business. Some do not want to change, but we can at least try. God can't make us change, but he gives us the ability to change. If someone as ate up as me can change, anyone can change.

After five years of serving God, my life has much changed. I no longer need nerve pills. I feel God put me through the bad times so I could help others who are like me. I learned responsibility and the peace and pride of a good life. I have to consistently remind myself not to take a step back. Sin is fun, and it takes willpower and faith to keep one's heart clean.

Sadly, Jerry succumbed to pancreatic cancer and died in November 2008—way too soon in his new life.

Jerry's values and life turnaround began with getting a job so as to stay out of prison. He then found a partner who made him want to take more steps to climb back up the ladder. But, the final act that hard wired the good things he had learned and got rid of the bad things that remained was finding a church and learning what belief in God could cause him to do. Famous and admired people, along with average people, or folks like Jerry, have turned their lives and values around with help from religion and God.

While finding God was a significant turnaround for many and would certainly be helpful to anyone in this mode, it is not the only way.

Condoleezza Rice, former secretary of state, grew up in Birmingham, Alabama, surrounded by segregation and racial violence by people such as the Ku Klux Klan. Her parents saw that she got an education, and, as she puts it, "My parents had me absolutely convinced that, well, you may not be able to have a hamburger at Woolworth's, but you can be president of the United States." [29]

Oprah Winfrey's early growing up shifted north and south between mother, father, and grandmother. Her mother worked and she was left to be watched by her nineteen-year-old cousin. He raped her and she was also abused by a family "friend" and an uncle. With little guidance she began skipping school, stealing money from her mother, running away and becoming pregnant. At sixteen, she read the autobiography of Maya Angelou and began to get her life straightened out. With her speaking ability, she got a job in radio leading to a four-year college scholarship and a career path and life from radio, to television, to where she is today. [30]

Paul, the great Christian missionary, speaker, and major writer of the New Testament, did not start that way.

". . . he made havoc of the church, entering into every house, and hauling men and women committed them to prison." Then, he was shown the light and began his work for the Lord. (31)

Dr. Benjamin Carson, renowned head of pediatric neurosurgery at Johns Hopkins Children's Center, began life very differently:

His father left when he was 8. His mother, who only had a third grade education . . . held two or more menial jobs to support her two sons, Curtis and Ben. The family was poor and he often endured cruel taunts at school. He fell behind in his studies and became known as "the dummy" of his class. He had a violent temper and hurt a student at school and almost hit his mother with a hammer over what clothes to wear. When he brought home a failing report card his mother took action. She limited TV to only after homework was done. She set up a program for them to read two library books a week and write reports to her, which she could not read, but they did not know this. Carson moved from the bottom of his class to the top, but was shown resentment by his classmates in the nearly all white school. When he won an achievement award as a freshman, a teacher stood up and berated his white classmates for letting a person of color outshine them. Carson faced racism through high school. He graduated from Yale and went on to Michigan University. He is known for successfully performing difficult neurosurgery, done for the first time. He has a talented wife and family. (32)

My wife and I just watched the movie of his life, *Gifted Hands: The Ben Carson Story.* I guarantee that, no matter your current value status, if you watch the wonder of this film, you will be motivated to improve your life and those around you. Here are some other examples:

The Englishman, John Newton, went from the captain of a slave ship to an outstanding minister and wrote the beautiful hymn "Amazing Grace" and many others. (33)

Jesse Owens rose from being the son of a sharecropper and grandson of a slave to being the first Olympian to win four gold medals in the 1936 Olympics. Through speaking, he set the example for millions of young people and spent his life working with youth on the playgrounds in the poorest neighborhoods. (34)

Through pure luck, years ago, I happened to be traveling in a train coach with only one other passenger. I thought I knew who it was. I spoke with the conductor, and he said it was Jesse Owens. We spent some good time just talking.

If Jerry Louvier and these people can rise to these levels from such troublesome and modest beginnings, anyone—no matter his or her start in life—can do it. If you really need to make significant change in your life's values, you cannot sit and hope for some life-changing experience to rescue you. Find something positive in your life and the environment around you, no matter how small, and act on it. Go back to school. Identify the skills you have and find any constructive job. Seek counsel and help from any positively oriented relative, friend, or mentor you have. The church or organizations in your community are there to help you.

If you are a person with good values stuck in an abusive environment that is destroying your life, seek trusted help and "get out of Dodge." Then work with positive support folks and organizations to help you find those things that will improve your quality of life and strengthen your values.

Though not often publicized, we all know of athletes, business leaders, politicians, Hollywood celebrities, and the like who have used their talents to perform as positive role models, to lend support to others, and give honor to their chosen field. They applied themselves to develop a positive ethical set that would carry them in whatever they chose to do in life. On the other hand, we hear too much about those in similar positions who abused the opportunities their talents gave them. They kept or reverted to bad habits and friends, greed, or self-pleasure and misused the rewards they earned and were given. In the process, they destroyed the faith of those who looked up to them. Some in that position overcame like Jerry Louvier. No matter your station in life, you own your values and are endowed with free will in our society. No one can stop you from taking positive steps to keep or improve your values and the consistency of their application. Of course, only the law can keep you from the reverse.

Making Values Work

As an individual and a citizen, you can do the following things:

- Be conscious of and make your positive values a key input to your decisions, behavior, and relationships.
- Seek friends and situations that will reinforce the application of these values.
- When tempted, stick to your positive values.
- If one of your life's results is in trouble, seek help to gain the resolve to get out of it.
- Exercise your right to vote your convictions, but seek candidates who have produced results that demonstrate positive values and integrity.

As a family, you can do the following things:

- Establish and discuss personal and family values within the family.
- Discuss specific situations and how values should be applied, as well as temptations that could get in the way and how to handle them.
- Set up ways to discuss and share problems and successes in values application.
- Agree on appropriate penalties and rewards.
- Walk the talk and keep communication channels open.

So many people who stress the importance of the family have suggested that having dinner together is a key. That is a good place for these discussions. In our family, we did just that. Our children often had their friends be a part of our dinners together. I recently celebrated a major birthday, and my son Paul and his wife, Debbie, put together a wonderful book of remembrances from those who shared my life. Many of those friends of our sons—who shared our dinners and home—still recalled and commented on the impact of those discussions as their lives developed. That was very special.

As a leader of an organization, you can do the following things:

- Make sure your organization has positive, and clearly articulated basic beliefs.
- See that those beliefs give proper priority to employees, customers, and investors for long-term success.
- See that they are interpreted to cover new social, environmental, and global changes and opportunities.
- See that they are fully communicated for understanding down through your organization—make it known that staying with your fundamental purpose and basic beliefs is the key to future survival, growth, and profitability.
- Establish surveillance and controls to see that they are applied.
- Determine review mechanisms, rewards, and penalties.
- Make success in your organization dependent on the results from application of these beliefs.

As a professional, you can do the following things:

- Participate in and know the beliefs, values, and standards of conduct that guide your profession.
- Apply those values to your business and in all your client work.
- Do not do business with prospects, clients, or suppliers who expect you to violate your values.

- Make sure your personal values square with those professional ethical standards.
- Make sure your employees understand the rewards for application and penalties for violation.
- Find secure and confidential ways to see that significant violations of ethical standards by others in your profession are made known.

As a teacher, you can do the following things:

- Know and understand the values that drive and do not drive your organization.
- Help your students understand the importance of those values in their educational and personal progress and success.
- Help them understand the short and long-term consequences for repeated failure to apply them and the rewards when they do.
- Walk the talk, follow through, and keep communication channels open.
- Work with your administration to get more parent support and involvement.

As a student, you can do the following things:

- Know the values of your school along with your own.
- Find the right situations and relationships to improve those values that need it.
- Make those values drive your decisions, behavior, and relationships.
- When value-tempting possibilities confront you, do not rationalize the long-term consequences for the immediate gain.
- Keep communications open, and seek trusted and respected help when tempted.

As an employee in an organization, you can do the following:

- Know the basic beliefs of your organization.
- Make sure you know how those beliefs apply to your work.
- Know of secure ways to report value breakdowns that cause performance that would negatively affect your department, fellow employees, and job.
- If you find the organization's beliefs and activities are in conflict with what you know to be right, don't succumb. If you have to stay, try to get those organizational beliefs changed. Or get out of there if you can.

As a politician—one who is campaigning, elected, or appointed—you can do the following:

- Make your true values known, and how they have and will impact your decisions and behavior.
- Keep your word, and do not get sucked into any negative value culture that may exist where you govern.
- Do not subvert your values to horse-trading voting issues.
- Seek ways to influence colleagues in those same positive directions.
- Report back to your voters what you have and have not supported and how your values influenced those outcomes.
- If you are about to get involved in a values temptation with major potential consequences, seek trusted help, and don't do it.
- If you should get involved, admit it when it happened, stop it, take the consequences, and ask for forgiveness and another chance.

By now, you should have some good ideas for improving your values and their application. But those good intentions soon fade without action. I want this book to result in action. So, while this is fresh in your mind, I hope you will do a little self-improvement work. The following steps provide some easy ideas for what you could do. When you have a plan, it strengthens the motivation to put it to work. If you don't have a life plan, you are adrift!

In responding to the following guidelines, have in mind the various environments in which you live. They could include school, work, family, community/neighborhood, social activities, and the like. Also think about those who influence your life. These could include parents, family, relatives, teachers, friends, mentors, bosses, co-workers, religious leaders, and the like. Make sure you are honest with yourself in your responses.

Refer to your list of values in chapter 2 and the column "Standard of Excellence."

1. Select and list one value you know has too often produced unsatisfactory results in your important activities and responsibilities. Consider situations either at school or work or in the family or in the community.

   _____

2. Describe one of your important activities or responsibilities where the influence of that value has produced unsatisfactory results. Be specific about what was dissatisfying and what occurred as a result.

   _____
   _____
   _____
   _____

3. Restate that value from item 1 above to include a higher personal "standard of excellence."

   _____

4. With that restated value in mind, list what actions you could take to remove the dissatisfaction with that activity or responsibility in item 2 above so as to improve the results.

_____

_____

_____

_____

5. If there are other factors or conditions beyond the impact of your value that are also influencing those unsatisfactory results, describe them and what actions you could take to improve or eliminate those conditions.

_____

_____

_____

_____

Again, refer to your list of values in chapter 2 and the column "Standard of Excellence."

6. Select and list one value that has produced unsatisfactory results in your relationships with others. Consider situations at school or work or in the family or in the community.

_____

7. Describe a specific relationship where the impact of that value has produced unsatisfactory results. Be specific about what was dissatisfying and what occurred as a result.

_____

_____

_____

_____

8. Restate that value from item 6 above to include a higher personal "standard of excellence."

_____

9. With that restated value in mind, list what actions you could take to remove the dissatisfaction with the relationship in item 7 above so as to improve the results.

_____

_____

_____

_____

10. If there are other factors or conditions beyond the impact of your value that are also influencing your dissatisfaction with the relationship, describe them and what actions you could take to improve or eliminate those conditions.

_____

_____

_____

_____

Refer to your list of values in chapter 2 and the "Consistent Application" column.

11. Select and list one value you do not consistently apply to important decisions you make, often leading to unsatisfactory results.

_____

12. What actions could you take to more consistently apply that value to those decisions to improve the results?

_____

_____

_____

_____

13. If there are other factors or conditions beyond the impact of your value that are contributing to the unsatisfactory decision results, describe them and what actions you could take to improve or eliminate them.

_____

_____

_____

_____

Again, refer to your list of values in chapter 2 and the "Consistent Application" column.

14. Select and list one value you do not consistently apply to an important relationship you have with an individual or group, leading to unsatisfactory results.

_____

15. What actions could you take to more consistently apply that value to this relationship to improve results?

_____

_____

_____

_____

16. If there are other factors or conditions beyond the impact of your value that are contributing to the unsatisfactory results in this relationship, describe them and what actions you could take to improve or eliminate them.

———————————————————————————

———————————————————————————

———————————————————————————

———————————————————————————

You have begun the process of improving your values and their application. You will receive satisfaction, reward, and pride as you proceed. Hopefully that will make you want to carry on this effort with other activities, behaviors, and relationships. You can refer back to your list of values in chapter 2 and, for those you want to improve, determine the activities that would lead to improvement and better application.

This is not easy stuff. But, as my now deceased colleague, mentor, boss, and dear friend Ben Tregoe always counseled me in our creative work together, "Anything really worth doing is worth doing poorly." He paraphrased that from G. K. Chesterton: "If a thing is worth doing, it's worth doing badly." In other words, if the idea is good, don't wait around to perfect it. Do a little something with it, take it out into life, test and apply it, prove the worth of the idea, improve it—and the cycle never ends. Perfection is always in the next step ahead. But if you wait around for the perfect solution, you may never use the talents you have been given. So, get a start on your values, be it ever so small at the outset.

Now that you have begun shaping up your ethical standards and their application, it is time for the next and most rewarding opportunity anyone can have—that is to share one's principles and lifestyle with others who need that help and inspiration. That will improve the quality of their lives, and then they can share what they have learned with others in need. The potential groundswell that can result would halt the decline of our great American values and turn them upward—first, in your family and surroundings, then in your neighborhood/community, and finally across the United States. The future promise for America can be made secure for all who follow.

Chapter 4

THE GOLDEN RULE OF VALUES

These words express very well the intent I have for this book:

> For as much as government can do and must do, it is ultimately the faith and determination of the American people upon which this nation relies.

> Our challenges may be new. The instruments with which we meet them may be new. But those values upon which our success depends—hard work and honesty, courage and fair play, tolerance and curiosity, loyalty and patriotism—these things are old. These things are true. They have been the quiet force of progress throughout our history. What is demanded then is a return to these truths. What is required of us now is a new era of responsibility—a recognition on the part of every American that we have duties to ourselves, our nation, and the world, duties that we do not grudgingly accept but rather seize gladly, firm in the knowledge that there is nothing so satisfying to the character than giving our all to a difficult task.

> This is the price and promise of citizenship. [1]

While these words were spoken by President Obama in his inaugural address, I *do not* feel that he or his administration has fully lived up to them by their actions.

But, as he says, acting on these words goes far beyond the government. This is a necessity and responsibility each of us must accept if we are to bring America back to the proud nation it can be. This is not a responsibility to be escaped by "I don't have the time," "It's up to someone else," or "I don't know how to help." It is up to each one of us to get involved to the point where our conscience feels good.

In the previous chapter, we explored what we can do to improve our values and their application. With that plan in place, let's start on what we could do to spread and share those values and quality of life to organizations, groups, and individuals with values and improvement needs. It is time we took heed and acted on the adage that has always been true of our busiest people: those who do the most will always find time to do more for a just cause.

This chapter includes many examples of what organizations, groups, and individuals are now doing to conquer this challenge. Again, these are not included to overwhelm you, rather to intrigue you with the scope and depth of what is being done. Hopefully, that will light a fire.

These rules came from a book titled *50 Rules Kids Won't Learn in School* by Charles J. Sykes. They say a lot about sound values and why their application is important to high school graduates. They are called "11 things you will not learn in school":

1. Life is not fair—get used to it!
2. The world will not care about your self-esteem. The world will expect you to accomplish something BEFORE you feel good about yourself.

3. You will NOT make $60,000 a year right out of high school. You won't be a vice president with a car phone until you earn both.

4. If you think your teacher is tough, wait until you get a boss.

5. Flipping burgers is not beneath your dignity. Your grandparents had a different word for burger flipping: they called it opportunity.

6. If you mess up it is not your parents' fault, so don't whine about your mistakes, learn from them.

7. Before you were born, your parents were not as boring as they are now. They got that way from paying your bills, cleaning your clothes, and listening to you talk about how cool you thought you were. So before you save the rain forest from the parasites of your parents' generation, try delousing the closet in your own room.

8. Your school may have done away with winners and losers, but life HAS NOT.

9. Life is not divided into semesters. You don't get summers off and very few employers are interested in helping you FIND YOURSELF. Do that on your own time.

10. Television is NOT real life. In real life, people actually have to leave the coffee shop and go to jobs.

11. Be nice to nerds. Chances are you will end up working for one. (2)

Char and I recently watched the 2007 movie *Freedom Writers* on DVD. It was based on a true story from the book *The Freedom Writers Diary* by Erin Gruwell. It is the story of a new teacher who accepted Charles Sykes's rules. She was dropped into a class to teach freshman English in an inner-city school plagued by the most extreme violence and racial tensions you could imagine. Her students were totally unmotivated, uninvolved, warlike, disruptive, and presumed unteachable by the school hierarchy. With much perseverance, she developed innovative reading and writing projects that directly involved her students' lives and feelings. They were headed nowhere but now had desire to do better. Over the year, she turned those students from a very negative set of values and resulting troubled lives into core values to learn, accept and help each other, and see a future. She changed their lives. The Freedom Writers Foundation provides training for teachers and scholarships for deserving students. They have a website.

Another excellent example of a teacher/coach who believes in these rules is covered in the 2008 book *The Assist* by Neil Swidey.

It is the true story of Jack O'Brien, a basketball coach at Charleston High School in Boston. He causes black players to trek daily across town to play ball and absorb the values that go with it. They come from racial and narrow margin neighborhoods that are pulling them down. O'Brien is impossibly tough on court but nurturing off it—both are what turned these disadvantaged kids around. "No one ever helped a kid by feeling sorry for him and letting him make excuses. Hard work beats natural ability every time." The most reliable route out of poverty is college. In the last decade O'Brien has helped more than thirty of his players get to college—some to prestigious places like Bowdoin, some to big-time basketball programs like the University of Florida, and many others to more modest schools whose names end in "State." He did not succeed with all. A few players could not continue their upward, value-driven lives when they got beyond his leadership and nurturing. [3]

Feel-good, non-result-based, politically correct, nondisciplinary, and advancement-at-any-cost-based education does not support or build core principles that will help students successfully cope with life's challenges and realities.

Lance Martin of Roswell, Georgia, in a *Viewpoint* commentary says it this way:

> The best thing any of us can do to help other people and our country thrive is to live a responsible life . . . If there

is one thing this world needs now more than ever, it is more contributors, more producers, and more creators. The common good is not created through government policies. It is created through the growth and prosperity derived from the minds and abilities of individuals who have made the conscious decision to produce and achieve. Forcefully taking the intellectual capital of these achievers for no value in return and giving it to those who have chosen not to produce does not induce equality. It kills the engine of innovation and feeds the very implements of its destruction. [4]

I agree with his conclusion.

Ultimately, the consistent application of sound and uplifting values leads to lives filled with the satisfaction and reward for things well done—the fulfillment from a productive career, the love and respect of family, the pride for serving one's community and country, the joy of helping others in need, and the peace of a good night's sleep.

One thing men who father children need to do with any ethical principles they can muster is become fathers to their children who need them. Dennis Todd, PhD, a licensed school psychologist, says the following:

> "The Heritage Foundation reports that the rise in juvenile crime and violence is directly related to the rise in fatherless families. Over 30 years of study show significant social and moral damage to children in homes devoid of loving, involved fathers. In many of these cases, male children are more than twice as likely to engage in delinquent behavior, drop out of school, and gravitate to a life of immorality and lawlessness. Proper civil and moral behaviors are the result of parenting not lack of money or education." [5]

Mom and Dad's presence is central to kid's well-being. Mom and Dad bring different, but equally important value developments to their children. This mutual need can be summed up nicely: when moms see their young ones scrambling up a jungle gym they tend to call out, "Be careful." Dad's challenge is likely to be different: "Can you make it to the top?" [6]

Kids need both!

My nonprofessional conclusions are as follows:

- If you are single, do not have sex, or at least do not have unprotected sex. Wait to have babies until you are married or have a relationship with a "significant other" committed to marriage.
- When married, do not have children until you both have proven that your relationship is based on "solid" and not "liquid" love.
- If you have children and your marriage is showing signs of impending trouble, seek all the qualified help you can find to help preserve your marriage.
- If you are decent folks but your differences are irreconcilable, seek settlement alternatives so that both of you can positively contribute to the development of your children.
- If your marriage is dissolving because only one of the parties has some bad habits, make sure the settlement protects the children as much as possible.
- If you are the abused partner in a physically abusive marriage, seek a trusted friend or organization to help you, take the kids, get the hell out of Dodge, and find a secure and protective environment to bring back your life.
- If you are a single parent, seek quality relatives, friends, and organizations to help you and your children with the counter role to your gender.

Activities for kids growing up today are much more organized than they were when we were kids. While there are many advantages to more organized activities, some good principles get downplayed in the process.

When we were kids, as boys, we created our own activities and fun. We played kick the can; had homemade rubber gun battles (made from old inner tube slices, a stick of wood, and a clothespin); formed armies and had pretend wars with other neighborhood armies; hiked through a farmer's field into the woods and made a fire to roast hot dogs; hiked to the old sandpit and figured out how to climb its steep walls; swam in the quarry; built and flew balsa wood model planes; walked to the park to swing, slide, and use the "monkey climber"; made a photo lab in the basement and developed films and prints for money; took apart old cars and fixed them; played "work up" baseball; basketball and "horse"; iced the blocked-off hill road and had sled competitions on the way down the hill; and much more. We learned teamwork, competition, leadership, equality, and fair play, and we discovered the good things about doing right and the consequences of doing wrong. My mom only insisted on knowing where I was and that I knew what time to come home—though she was curious about what I might be doing. Girls planned their own activities and fun.

Did all kids do those things? I think most did. Did they all end up with sound ethics and the good life? Of course not! There were bullies, tough guys, bad losers, overly competitive winners, and wimps. That will always be the case. But I don't recall—some say it was hidden—much teenage pregnancy, binge drinking, obesity, school shootings, illegal drug use, and the like. We can't go back, but we could seek a little better balance between lifestyles developed through organized activities and those developed through self-created activities.

While we got into mischief now and then, my memory says those were mainly creative, value-testing adventures. I know times have changed; families are busier, child safety is a concern, well-led and organized activities have merit, and the like. But, I am reminded of an example I read about in a book titled *Where Did You Go? Out. What Did You Do? Nothing* by Robert Paul Smith. A father had dropped off his son—in his uniform—for a Little League baseball practice. He got a little farther along and decided it would be fun to go back and watch the practice and see his son play. When he got back to the field, the boys were all sitting on the bench. He asked his son why they weren't playing, and his son replied, "Only eight of us showed up, and you need nine guys to make a team." We used to play "work up" when any four of us were around—one to pitch, bat, play infield, and play outfield—and you "worked up" to get to bat.

John Rosemond, previously quoted, says:

> It has long been my contention that children who grew up in the 1950s and '60s were much better behaved than today's kids. Don't misunderstand me. We were far from perfect. We misbehaved, of course, but most of the bad stuff we did was nothing more than mischievous, especially when compared with what kids are doing today. I didn't cheat because I was afraid—petrified is more like it—of what would happen if I was caught. Today, what's to fear? In fact, a teacher who has the nerve to give a cheater a failing grade might wind up in trouble. School administrators and teachers tell me today's kids don't really seem to care if they're caught. That is because, I'm told, they have no fear of adults or consequences. I suppose this is because adults no longer give children reason to fear them or what they might do. The problem really isn't kids. Kids have always tried to get away with what they could. The problem is adults who are having a problem saying cheating is just plain wrong, that there is no excuse for it. [7]

The parent/child/family message seems clear: good behavior standards, discipline, and values begin early and at home.

advice! Parents who take advantage of organized activities and
lso play with their little ones, read to them, and allow them to play
their own toys with time for themselves raise children who develop
? own creativity, self-confidence, and eagerness for learning.

1d, here is a book that can help.

William J. Bennett, author and former secretary of education
for President Reagan, has written a delightful book on the moral
education of youth. It is titled *The Book of Virtues.* It is filled with
stories and parables to help understand various ethical practices.
It would make good reading and discussion for parents and
older children. Reading it to younger kids would provide great
opportunities for dialogue:

He says of compassion: "A natural feeling which, by moderating
the love of self in each individual, contributes to the preservation
of the whole species." And of responsibility: "Responsible persons
are mature people who have taken charge of themselves and their
conduct, who own their actions and own up to them—who answer
for them." About friendship, he says: "In our age, when casual
acquaintance often comes so easily, and when intimacy comes
too soon and too cheaply, we need to be reminded that genuine
friendships take time. They take effort to make and work to keep."
Work he characterizes as: "Life's greatest joys are not what come
apart from the work of one's life, but with the work of one's life." His
stories of these values and others illustrate the rewards for positive
application and the consequences for the reverse. [8]

Next to family, the environment in which one grows up and lives
probably has the second-greatest impact on the decisions, behavior,
and relationships that develop and sustain the quality of one's
values and life. The members of the community, local government,
commercial organizations, and religious and societal organizations
all play a part in the quality of a community. When any or all are
weak or take their eyes and ears off the pulse, bad things can start

to happen. There is overdevelopment and sprawl; drugs, crime, and prostitution take over; businesses fail or leave; "good" folks who are able to do so move away; school quality declines; and poverty and dependence grow. Tonyaa Weathersbee reports in the *Florida Times-Union* the consequences on one life stuck in that environment:

> It is easy enough, for example, to say that a young man who receives a harsh sentence for selling drugs deserves it because it was irresponsible for him to commit a crime. But, if that young man lives in a world where joblessness abounds, and where drug dealers have turned his neighborhood into their company town, then his sense of personal responsibility is not going to be shaped by laws that make more sense for people living in places governed by the presence of legitimate work. His definition of personal responsibility is, more likely, going to turn on what he needs to do to survive. [9]

Turning those communities around will reduce criminal behavior, but in so doing, we must think of sound virtues and take minor offenders out of jails and instead place them into quality therapy and skills training. Along with that, we need to extend the sentences of very serious offenders who ruin lives of others for profit. Building more jails to satisfy our immediate concern and satisfaction about crime and criminals is not the answer. It is not corrective and leads only to more severe problems in the future.

In his book, *Code of the Streets: Decency, Violence, and the Moral Life of the Inner City*, Elijah Anderson contrasts:

". . . white middle-class sensibilities about "decency" and fatherhood, with the factually limited avenues available for success to young black males coming from broken homes and broken schools, the two primary institutions of socialization available to successful residents of the middle class. Solid schools and families, of course, provide the most powerful form of social control that there is: a well-cultivated but individually held social expectation of achievement. Informal social control of the sort exerted by families, coaches, religious leaders or engaging good teachers, in the end, comprises the real "glue" of society. The subtext of this debate about violence concerns who is most to blame: it's the mayor's fault, it's the rap musician's fault, it's the selfish white man's fault, it's the gun industry's fault, it's the black man's fault, or it's the parent's fault." We need to work together to build our way out of this. [10]

I thought this was a good approach to helping released, nonviolent prisoners like drug users not return to jail. This was published on the front page in our paper on May 17, 2010.

Jacksonville, FL is following the lead of many states to implement a court lead—Post Conviction Drug Court—program that helps ex-convicts reenter society. The voluntary program targets those considered at risk of failing traditional supervised release after prison. In addition to meeting with their probation officers, participants meet weekly with the judge who reviews their drug testing results, job and family relationships, and educational efforts. Those succeeding attend every other week and if they complete the yearlong program a year is knocked off their probation. Those who falter have more frequent court visits and serious violations can result in expulsion and return to prison. Results to date are encouraging as far as education, jobs, family connections, and self-worth. [11]

To show you how far our Puritan "out of sight, out of mind" heritage has permeated our genes, this article was published on the front page of that paper four days later on May 21, 2010.

"Duval County (Jacksonville) court officials have notified the state they are shutting down post-conviction drug court—and rejecting $1.4 million in grant money that came with it—because of opposition by the State Attorney's Office. When Zarle (drug court coordinator Kelly Zarle) wrote in January that it is more costly to incarcerate drug offenders 'only for them to come out and re-offend,' Assistant State Attorney Sandra Rosendale fired back: 'I disagree with you, all due respect, but I think they should just build more prisons.'" Professor Michael Hallett from the University of North Florida said, "Specialized courts like drug court have been proven to save money and lower recidivism. While it costs $25,000 to $30,000 a year to incarcerate inmates in Florida, in drug court they can be treated for $3,500." [12]

Sadly, the experimental program was thrown out before any real results could be shown. With all the money and effort that has gone into reducing our illegal drug problem, results have been few and far between. While the debate goes on, I am now convinced that, with proper controls, we should experiment with making illegal drugs legal. As far as I can see, the benefits to society far outweigh the consequences. Prohibition of alcohol did not work either.

Those who have been very successful in sports, the theater, business, the professions, and the arts are in an ideal position to share the values that guided their activities and behavior to help those who lack ethical standards with unsatisfactory results. There are countless creative ways to make this happen. Shaquille O'Neal provides an excellent example.

He learned many important lessons about helping others from his father as he was growing up. From that, here are some of the things he is now doing: "Shaq-a Claus" which started with forming a partnership with Toys "R" Us to each donate $30,000 for toys to kids in a homeless shelter who would not receive gifts for Christmas; "Shaqsgiving" where he joins force with local food banks to feed families at Thanksgiving; Make-A-Wish where 20 people have been put through four-year nursing schools; support for Boys and Girls Clubs of America—"as a kid they helped me become what I am." And he dreams big—"I would like to take over school lunch programs for the whole country and call it 'Shaquille Meals.' Another dream is to get big-name people to do a 50-state telethon at Christmas.

It has always been my theory that people with influence can help make the world a better place." [13]

Patricia Kime reports what some others are doing to help those in need:

> Michael Apodaca, son of 2000 National Honoree Maida Apodaca, and a dozen volunteers will travel from El Paso, TX, to Juarez, Mexico, to build a house for an impoverished family. Kylie Kuhns, 13, of Mifflinburg, PA, is holding a kickball tournament to raise money for her foundation, Kelsey's Dream, which provides snack boxes, blankets, and toys for sick children. In Durham, NC, 100 Durham Community Land Trustees volunteers will landscape and do home improvement projects for twenty families living in affordable housing. Veterans will be the focus for 100 Wilson Classical High School students in Long Beach, Calif., as they make 50 quilts for distribution to the state's Veterans Affairs Hospitals. [14]

Any citizen or group with love of our country and its future, sound values, and a reasonably successful life can create or join a program that will make a difference for those in need. It is time to take that challenge!

If your community is in trouble, the Harlem Children's Zone (HCZ) is a program that civic leaders, support organizations, and members of your community should be interested to track.

"Called 'one of the most ambitious social-service experiments of our time' by the *New York Times*, the Harlem Children's Zone Project is a unique, holistic approach to rebuilding a community so that its children can stay on track through college and go on to the job market. The goal is to create a 'tipping point' in the neighborhood so that children are surrounded by an enriching environment of college-oriented peers and supportive adults, a counter weight to 'the street' and a toxic popular culture that glorifies misogyny and anti-social behavior. The two fundamental principles of the zone project are to help kids as early in their lives as possible and to create a critical mass of adults around them who understand what it takes to help children succeed. HCZ also works to reweave the social fabric of Harlem, which has been torn apart by crime, drugs and decades of power." It has helped hundreds of families convert their city-owned buildings to tenant-owned coops. [15]

The organization began in 1970. In 1997, the HCZ began a network of programs for a twenty-four-block area and in 2007 the Zone Project grew to almost 100 blocks and served 7,400 children and over 4,100 adults. "Over the years, the agency introduced several ground-breaking efforts: in 2000, the Baby College parenting workshops; in 2001, the Harlem Gems pre-school program; also in 2001, the HCZ Asthma Initiative, which teaches families to better manage the disease; in 2004, the Promise Academy, a high-quality public charter school; and in 2006, an obesity program to help children stay healthy. All HCZ programs are offered free to the children and families of Harlem, which is made possible by donations from people like you." [16]

> HCZ Educational results are encouraging. 100% of students in Harlem Gems pre-K program were found to be school-ready for the sixth year in a row. 81% of Baby College parents improved the frequency of reading to their children. HCZ Promise Academy II scored at or above grade level in the state-wide math test. A few blocks away 97% of the Promise Academy I third graders were at or above grade level. [17]

HCZ has created the Practitioners Institute which shares information about their work with others. "The goal is to help communities so they can identify their resources and needs, and then organize a coordinated, interdisciplinary strategy. For a reasonable fee a community delegation can attend either a three-hour or three-day workshop." [18]

Jacksonville has begun such a program called New Town Success Zone.

As with the Harlem project, the idea is to start with a small area and flood it with social services. It is located in a small defined poverty/ crime area with 5,000 adults and 1600 children. Community leaders from Jacksonville and the local community, businesses, city government, and all existing social service organizations are coordinating their efforts to put programs in place to bring low-income kids up to speed, and charter schools, with longer hours, are being developed. Rampant drug dealing is being cleared out to create a feeling of safety for families and their children. [19]

Communities that need help don't have to wait around until outside forces organize to help them. The Reverend Nelson Johnson, president of the Justice Fund in Greensboro, North Carolina, says this:

"Why now, do we have one neighborhood after another neighborhood, in every city and every state, with black people hanging on by their fingernails, with drugs as the economy in the community, and homeless shelters growing by leaps and bounds?" He runs a center that not only provides sustenance, but provides job training and seeks jobs. He adds, "Work is what you do to grow your own gifts. If they were working, their whole sense of themselves would change. And if more people in struggling black communities decided to become more involved in plotting their own destinies, a lot of other things could change as well." [20]

You can organize and do this in neighborhoods around you that need help. That will raise the entire area's quality of life.

Students need a voice in efforts to improve communities.

High school and college students, when asked by a Youth Development Committee, stressed the need for quality after-school programs and mentors that are genuinely interested. Sadly, one student said that mentors in an after-school program she attended were more like babysitters than teachers or mentors. Social skills and self-esteem need development by positive role models who can help offset the negative media images where violence and drugs are glorified. They spoke at length about self-esteem issues confronting inner-city youth faced with economic strife and parents who too often are self-centered or strung out on drugs and drop the ball on raising their children. President Claudette Williams of Edward Waters College summed it up. "A caring, significant adult in a child's life makes the difference." [21]

The press has written about the need for more mentoring of those students who lack the parental support they need, and the results are showing in their school progress and behavior. While any good citizen can become involved, this is a program where businesses with local facilities like Comcast are in an ideal position to significantly expand support and get involved.

Thirty-three Sandalwood High School students were paired with thirty-three Comcast employees Thursday to see what they could accomplish in a Big Brothers Big Sisters mentoring program called Beyond School Walls. Unlike other mentoring programs in Jacksonville schools, the Littles will visit with their Bigs, most of them senior Comcast managers, every two weeks in the Comcast workplace for the rest of the school year. Comcast plans to use social media such as Facebook so the Littles can keep in touch with what they are doing in the program. "Student comments: Billy said he believes he will gain a lot from the matchup and get an intelligent business view; Anna, a 10th grade student, said she tries to keep focused on school and what she needs to do to become a responsible adult; and Will, an 11th grader, says I'm looking forward to gaining some real life job experience." [22]

Think how many mentors could be provided if all businesses took up this easy-to-organize activity!

There are strong and compelling feelings about budget allocations that affect community life and values. Tonyaa Weathersbee, a columnist for the *Florida Times-Union*, provides a case in point. She comments about crime, prison, and public education:

In a year of crippling budget cuts, the state plans to spend nearly $300 million on new prisons while public education will lose more than $300 million. And no one seems to care about that. She also cites the creation of the Florida lottery whose billions were to enhance and inspire the public education system beyond the state's operating budget that covered education's basics. But instead of using the lottery for real enhancement, lawmakers soon began reducing education's share of the operating budget necessitating lottery money to make up the difference. She says there is a fix: a new political alliance made up of poor and middle-class parents sick of resource-strapped schools, lawmakers who fought the education cuts and decent citizens who understand that crime prevention through education is a better long-term investment than incarceration. [23]

I am sure many communities need mentors for their students who lag behind and citizen watchdogs to make sure school budgets are appropriate and directly allocated to student education. If enough folks got involved in those activities, that just might be enough to cure some of public education's significant problems!

On the other hand, sometimes good things happen to communities in need when government gets involved along with societal and civic leaders.

Twelve of eighteen Duval County high schools support graduation rates of 60% or less. So, in tough economic times the Jacksonville City Council approved a $32.3 million anti-crime package. Among that package educational projects included: 25 new early learning centers across the city; five out-of-school suspension centers; expansion of a successful middle school to take 2,800 more students. Beyond that, thousands of volunteer mentors are needed for the school system—they fill a gap in a child's life and provide the encouragement and support to motivate the child to stay in school. [24]

Any state, county, or local government can apply values that find a little money to take out of current activities and invest it in long-range community stability and survival. Make a start, and watch it grow and produce results. Citizens might even pay a little more for your dedication to this effort.

There are unlimited opportunities to volunteer our time, skills, and dollars to improve our own communities/neighborhoods/cities. We don't have to focus our efforts just within high-poverty areas, although that is a good place to start. Improving the environment, infrastructure, commerce, and quality of life across the entire city leads to higher expectations for all who live there. Just cleaning up the city raises hopes and encourages folks to make better things happen. Public and private social service organizations, schools, city commissions, and the like need volunteers and mentors to improve the quality of life across the areas they serve. Conditions like many of those in chapter 1 will not be addressed—and our collective values uplifted accordingly—any other way.

While it takes many to turn a community or a city around, often that process must start with a strong and dedicated leader. The efforts of Mayor Rudolph Giuliani in New York City are an outstanding example.

When he was elected in 1993 over one million were on welfare—every 7th resident. He initiated the country's largest "workforce" program and over the next 8 years 691,000 people moved from welfare to work and self-sufficiency. Computer mapping allowed the police to focus their efforts on high-violence/crime locations. In two years serious crime was reduced by over one third and murder by one half. While many attributed the crime drop to an improved economy, it continued down during an economic downturn. Public shootings declined 40%, violence in city jails by 95%, and the crime rate by 57%. The FBI rated New York as America's safest city. He also eradicated the influence organized crime had on commerce. Hundreds of millions of dollars siphoned off by racketeers was returned to the business sector. Income and property values rose and whole neighborhoods were re-developed. With the improvement in the economy he turned a $2.3 billion budget deficit into a multi-billion dollar surplus. [25]

We profess extremely low trust in our elected federal government officials, but we reelect more than 80 percent of the incumbents. So, the conflict between trust and who we elect is up to voters to resolve. Perhaps current voter anger and frustration and movements like the Tea Party protests will shake up enough voters to change this pattern. Whether Democrat, Republican, or Independent, it's time we sought and elected candidates who have demonstrated a positive and consistent application of ethical principles—who are dedicated enough to stand against the Washington political culture and whose votes will not be swayed by earmarks and voting trade-offs. Those we elect to the federal government must candidly debate, reach agreement, and act on those major, long-term, national issues that will assure survival of our republic.

The same point holds at state and local levels. It is easiest to turn this negative political system around at the local/county level where voters know the issues and the candidates, can track results, and organize change. For most of us, that is a good place to start. As our community governance and results improve, that can collectively spread to state and federal levels as those candidates get the message.

American business, whether large, midsized, or small, can do a lot to provide the scope of leadership and resources to turn values in the right direction. They can help bring back sound principles to communities in many ways. In this fast-changing and competitive world, they have much to gain from those efforts. To start, they need positive internal codes of behavior to drive their business decisions. Then, they can use their power and resources where they are located to help the local community and those in need.

John Coxwell grew up in a small town with sound ethical practices and far from inner-city issues and violent crime. That stood him in good stead and, now in Jacksonville; he heads up the Targeted Intervention and Rehabilitation Subcommittee of the Jacksonville Journey program. Their assignment is to address needs of those who have made mistakes and help them find ways back to a responsible life. As the head of J. B. Coxwell Contracting Inc., he hires former felons who want to change: folks who have seen the inside of prison and don't want to go back. He says, "The former convicts who work for me are model employees who have learned the hard way that crime doesn't pay, and are committed to honest work. There are thousands of men and women—people who have paid their debt to society and want to do the right things but need a hand getting started. Giving them a chance to prove themselves is one great way to stop the "revolving door" of justice and improve their lives and our city. Positive role models and opportunities in neighborhoods can make the difference, keeping them off the streets and out of trouble. In reading this you could be thinking it's a great idea, but it doesn't have anything to do with me. You're not right. Wherever you live, this is your problem. If you own a business or hire people, employ rehabilitated felons; get your church or civic group to partner with a closed community center; be a mentor, coach or tutor and promote strong ethics in your corner of town. [26]

Give Back Getaways and VolunTeaming is a new nationwide initiative by the Ritz-Carlton Group of hotels. It provides local volunteering opportunities to leisure guests, group clients, and employees. "It's easy and fun, and it takes only a few hours to obtain a deep sense of satisfaction while impacting the lives of children for years to come." For example, the Ritz-Carlton of Amelia Island partners with the Boys and Girls Club of Nassau County. Growing Green pairs volunteers with kids to plant a tree, arrange a flower bed, and the like. Brain Power Hour gives volunteers a chance to work with kids on math, spelling, and the like. Fit Kids give volunteers a chance work with kids to coach a soccer game or other sports activity. Corporate groups can work with kids to build and beautify a playground. One group bought and filled 200 backpacks with school supplies. A recent guest said, "We're all so busy in our day-to-day lives, and knowing that I can take a few hours and do something to help a child while I am on vacation makes my stay even more enjoyable and meaningful. I think it is a great idea." [27]

Harris Rosen owns seven hotels in Orlando. He uses his wealth and time to revitalize Tangelo Park, a once drug-infested, trouble-plagued community of 2,400 near his hotels. He provides pre-school education for all 2-3-4 year old children and a college education for all high school graduates in Tangelo Park. Crime has fallen 67% and the high school dropout rate from 25% to 6%. Rosen feels if he could get any wealthy person to visit this community, they would go back home and follow his lead. He also feels charitable giving is much more rewarding if one is personally involved. While most wealthy giving goes to good causes like colleges, foundations, museums, and hospitals, that will be of questionable value if we don't salvage the neighborhoods where crime and ignorance fester. Rosen recognizes that these kinds of problems give rise to pathological behavior that threatens to turn our society into an archeological dig. [28]

So, if you are very wealthy, think about giving some of your charity dollars and time to this kind of value-improving project. If you are "sort of" wealthy—or just middle class—consider bringing your friends together and planning such a project.

Most local business executives and leaders have sound values which guide their personal and company decision making and behavior. We need many more of them to step up and emulate the volunteer efforts of John Coxwell, the Ritz-Carlton Hotel, and Harold Rosen. That could create a huge value/result-turning outcome.

The *Kiplinger Letter* reports how employers feel about public education and what should be done to improve it:

"Employers are grabbing the education baton and running hard. They want: Congress to refocus the No Child Left Behind Act more on high school. Companies also want full funding of the America Competes Act, a law passed last year authorizing new federal investments for technology, math, and engineering education, including teacher training." As far as education, business seeks a major overhaul at state and local levels:

- Programs to improve teaching and management and create innovative curricula;
- Better data to identify and then reward the best teachers;
- Smaller classes;
- More advanced courses for top students;
- Superintendents held accountable for their performance. [29]

One hundred companies have gone together to form "Step Up For Students"—a scholarship program for low-income family students to attend a private high school. 22,000 K-12 students are in the program. Denisha Merriweather was a dropout candidate failing all her third grade subjects. She is now an honor student at her private school with a 3.8 grade point and has plans for college [30]

"By 2016, nearly 80% of all US jobs will require more than a high school diploma, but 70 million Americans between the ages of 25 and 40 haven't gone past grade 12. In fact, the US is the only industrialized country where the generation entering the workforce is less educated than the one leaving it, though Germany is getting close to that point." Business, along with a variety of private foundations, is tackling the challenge to improve workforce education by sponsoring mentoring programs, internships, and funding community colleges. [31]

American business is also helping improve society by expanding its value set beyond those relating just to its products, customers, employees, investors, and legality. It is called corporate social responsibility (CSR). It has always been there, but in the past was good for public relations, particularly if there had been a misstep by a company along the way. Now, it goes way beyond just good public relations. It is part of the DNA of the value set of any corporation seeking sustainability and survivability in the years ahead. While there is debate about how far the "greening" and community action of business should go, it is happening with increasing frequency. Opponents argue that the function of business is to grow its revenue and profits so as to provide research dollars for innovation, to create jobs, and to reward investors. Proponents argue that CSR does just that over the long term. They say business needs a public relations shot in the arm—that going green, having a community conscience, and applying sound ethical principles preserves our environment over the long term, attracts the new generation Y workers, creates American jobs, improves the communities where a company operates and their reputation, and, done right, is sustaining and profitable.

A study of five thousand current MBA students by Universum USA in Philadelphia reported the following:

While top job choices were the usual consulting companies, typical manufacturing and service-oriented companies moved well up the choice ladder. "Why the change?" The explanation, according to Tattanelli (CEO of Universum USA): "This is a group with new priorities, specifically, a desire for their work to have a meaningful social purpose, and to be employed by companies that appear to have high ethical standards." [32]

Broadening corporate America's values for new environmental outreach does not have to be just goodwill:

Waste Management is the leading converter of waste to energy, operating 17 plants that process 24,000 tons of a waste per day providing power to more than one million homes and saving 14 million barrels of oil per year. It operates 100 landfill gas-to-energy projects that turn methane into clean energy. From its landfills it provides 17,000 acres of protected land for wetlands and wildlife sanctuary. Their goal is to show consumers they are linking everyday collection to environmental protection. That should attract and sustain new customers far into the future. GE's high-profile commitment to "Ecomagination" to innovate in product and package design, water stewardship, greenhouse gas mitigation, product life-cycle analysis, solar powered locomotives, lower emission aircraft engines, and more efficient lighting should produce exciting new product/market/profit projects. Domtar has become a leader in developing products using the most comprehensive and rigorous sustainable forestry standards in existence. Its certification by the Forest Stewardship Council gives its products a competitive advantage as its customers can communicate their commitment to conservation. [33]

Starbucks Coffee Company's Howard Schultz and Jim Donald say this:

> We have always believed that leadership companies must set a higher standard for how business is done. And we want to assure you that we remain committed to our core values and our vision to do business in a different way—a way that creates long-term value for our shareholders while honoring the contributions of the farmers and our people who make our success possible. Our approach to corporate social responsibility (CSR) includes developing ethical sourcing practices for products such as coffee and cocoa, strengthening our involvement in education programs focused on cultural diversity globally, funding water projects in developing countries, and reducing our environmental footprints. For thirty-five years it has remained our goal

to show that running a profitable business and being a good neighbor aren't mutually exclusive; that, with focused attention, a little extra effort and an overriding desire to do the right thing a company can enjoy financial success while being a socially responsible corporate citizen. [34]

Patagonia, a $270 million company producing outdoor clothing and equipment, is a prime and unique example of a company extending its values to the greening movement. It is privately held by its founder, Yvon Chouinard.

He says no to anything that would compromise his values. Back in 1997, Chouinard wanted to find out which materials caused the most harm to the environment? Conventional cotton was the most heinous, dependent on noxious pesticides, insecticides, and defoliants. He said, "To know this and not switch to organic cotton was unconscionable." In 1994, he gave his managers 18 months to make the change. Given that organic cotton was rare, cost 50% to 100% more, and was one fifth of his business, there was no small risk. It paid off and his cotton sales grew 25% developing an organic cotton industry. Other companies crossed over and in 2006 Walmart became the world's largest purchaser of organic cotton. In early 2000, he wanted to find out if the product itself could be recycled? When Chouinard's Japanese partner found a way to recycle polyester, he had customers return used polyester products and saved 76% of the energy from making it from virgin petroleum. While he graduated from auto mechanics in high school he is now a standing-room only ticket at Stanford and Harvard Business Schools. [35]

That is a great start but we have a long way to go. Think what it would do if every business leader had a value set like Howard Schultz, Jim Donald, and Yvon Chouinard and the creativity, courage, and conviction to find ways to have his or her company right our environmental course and help secure our future.

Helping Youth Improve

Jake Posey got hooked on Big Brothers Big Sisters when he read how rewarding that experience would be and how much impact it had on boys and girls. He is paired with Brannon Dalton and they have fun hanging out on weekends whether fishing, playing in the park, or looking for shark's teeth. It is not just fun, as they do community projects such as beach cleanup and dog walking for the animal shelter. Brannon has learned to enjoy them and also knows he can count on Jake to be there when he needs him. [36]

While that program takes a little heavier time commitment, I am involved with another worthwhile program that requires less time on my part but is just as rewarding. It is a program titled Take Stock in Children. It is state supported and operates in every county in Florida. Its mission is to provide a tuition-free scholarship to any Florida public college or university for achieving middle and high school students from low-income families. Many of those families are headed by single parents. In the seventh grade, the student signs a pledge to not smoke, drink, or take drugs, maintain at least a 2.5 grade point average, be a good citizen, and not get in legal trouble through graduation. I mentored one such student. I was thoroughly checked out and received appropriate training. The program called for us to meet for one hour a week during the school year at his school. I was to be his friend and help him stay the course to graduation. This is a program through which any caring adult with good values can help an achieving young person improve his or her school experience, values, and chances for success in life. II. I have finished the sixth year of mentoring my student and he has graduated from high school. He is now a sophomore in college. He comes from a home headed by a single mother. He turned from a shy underachiever who often missed school and homework assignments to an outgoing, mainly-A-and-B student who is excited about going to college. Though not an official part of the Take Stock in Children program, I will continue to work with him as a friend and counselor throughout his college experience and his life. He has a sound code of ethics and has the intelligence, drive, and maturity to make it through college and into a successful career and life. He will be the first person in his family to receive a college degree. He and I both know that this program and our relationship is a key to maintaining his motivation to move from a fatherless and poverty-oriented environment to an enriching and self-fulfilling career and life. And, second best, my rewards have paralleled his!

I have some concern about all the nationwide effort on the need for a four-year college degree and a professional life. Sometimes, I think we have made young folks who don't or can't aspire to that direction feel second rate. Jobs for highly trained service providers, skilled trade and vocational workers, technical and administrative support folks, health care workers, and the like used to be well respected and sought after. These are well-paying and essential jobs. We need much more encouragement and support for young folks to obtain the advanced training and certification to qualify for these positions. They will provide satisfying and rewarding careers. While some may debate it, there is increasing support for this point of view:

"The notion that a four-year degree is essential for real success is being debated by a growing number of economists, policy analysts, and academics. They say more Americans should consider other options such as technical training or two-year schools." As evidence they cite rising student debt, stagnant graduation rates, and a struggling job market flooded with overqualified degree-holders. For example, Kate Hodges, a college town high school senior with a 3.5 grade point, a college savings account, and a family tree full of advanced degrees is headed to the Tulsa Oklahoma Welding School to earn an associate's degree in welding technology. Martin Scaglione, president of work force development for ACT, suggested, "Nothing short of a new definition for educational success is needed to diminish the public bias toward four-year degrees." [37]

There are many charitable organizations that help youth in need. Significantly increasing the scope and impact of these organizations is perhaps the easiest way to turn our declining values tide. If we can't save this generation, we can save the next one. Here are a few to pique your interest and potential involvement.

The Boys and Girls Clubs of America operate 4,300 clubs nationwide serving 4.8 million boys and girls from early childhood through teen age. Its purpose is to help a generation at risk through homework improvement, nutritional help, sports and recreational activities, and academic programs. [38]

Communities in Schools has programs nationwide in twenty-seven states serving two million young people through two hundred local affiliates. Its purpose is to help students stay in school, to help communities assess the needs of their youth and design plans for meeting those needs with existing community resources, and connecting young people with those services in a variety of ways. [39]

Retired & Senior Volunteer Program (RSVP) serves 329,000 children and youth per year through its Foster Grandparents Program for volunteers over sixty years of age. Its purpose is to help the most vulnerable children in the United States through tutoring, mentoring, help, and support. [40]

Junior Achievement has 384,000 volunteers who teach 367,000 classes to 9,300,000 students a year. JA Worldwide is the world's largest organization dedicated to educating students (K-12) about workforce readiness, entrepreneurship, and financial literacy through experiential, hands-on programs. [41]

Boy Scouts of America has 792,000 scouts and 494,000 leaders:

> Boy Scouts of America is one of the nation's largest and most prominent values-based youth development organizations. The BSA provides a program for young people that builds character, trains them in the responsibilities of participating citizenship and develops personal fitness. [42]

I can vouch for the good work done by the Boy Scouts. At one point, my son Paul worked for them and still helps when needed on a volunteer level. His two sons, David and Will, are both Eagle Scouts and fine young men.

The Girl Scouts has 2.3 million scouts:

> Girl Scouting helps girls develop their full individual potential; relate to others with increasing understanding, skill, and respect; develop values to guide their actions and provide the foundation for sound-decision making; and contribute to the improvement of society through their abilities, leadership skills, and cooperation with others. [43]

Beyond these few examples, there are many other national, state, and local organizations dedicated to improving the values and lives of young people in need—organized athletics like Little League for baseball, church youth activities, school clubs and after-school programs, neighborhood clubs and recreational activities, youth centers, youth camps, YMCA activities, and many more. Find one that fits your interest and experience and give it your help.

While it is much more difficult to change values and mature adult behavior, that is part of our challenge for America's future.

Help for Adults in Need

I worked with Habitat for Humanity for ten years, helping them bring good principles to building homes for families that live in substandard housing and have limited incomes. The future owner must contribute several hundred hours to the construction and be able to pay an interest-free mortgage provided by local Habitat-raised funds. It was a fabulous experience, and I got to know some great volunteers. For all of us, it was a unique emotional high to see a family that never had a home receive their keys. All the results are local and help clean up and revitalize neighborhoods that need it. It is a very desirable program that permanently changes lives—it's not a handout but a hand up. It takes simple construction skills that you can bring or learn. This is a nationwide and worldwide program with each local affiliate needing help to pound nails, raise funds, and work on committees and the board. This is a value-building effort that anyone from a teenager to a senior citizen, male and female, can share. Most groups work on Saturdays, so working folks and those in school can get involved. Beyond your personal involvement, get the organization you work for or the church youth group you belong to or your family or neighbors to send a team and take some major responsibility for building one home.

Again, there are many organizations dedicated to helping families and adults in need. Here are a few more examples to stimulate your potential interest.

Catholic Charities operates nationwide with 240,000 volunteers and staff serving 7.8 million people of all faiths per year:

> Catholic Charities also strives to strengthen families and build stronger communities by offering a variety of other programs such as counseling, immigration and refugee services, adoption, disaster response, child care, employment training, support for seniors, and much more.[44]

Points of Light was a federal government program created in 1999 to cultivate volunteerism. At the same time, HandsOn Network was a grassroots creation to find new ways to volunteer. When they merged in 2007, HandsOn Network, with its 250 nationwide action centers and its affiliation with hundreds of nonprofit, community, government, and faith-based organizations, became the action arm for its work. [45]

RSVP, through its Senior Companion Program, serves almost one hundred thousand adults per year who have difficulty with simple tasks of living. For example, just in Itasca County in northern Minnesota, 784 Elder Circle volunteers provided 104,438 hours in 2008. They did things such as provide counsel on health insurance, shop for and deliver groceries, tutor students in reading, coach computer classes, and a myriad of other activities. RSVP also connects five hundred thousand folks over fifty-five to volunteer with service organizations in their communities that match their skills and interests. [46]

Students in Free Enterprise (SIFE) operates worldwide on fourteen hundred campuses in forty-eight countries with support from 250 major global corporations. Its purpose is to help students learn business leadership skills and, as a part of the program, use that knowledge to create economic opportunities for others in need. For example, students in California teach low-income women how to run day care centers. Over eight years, seven hundred have participated and about one-third have set up day care businesses and become self-sufficient. [47]

Beyond these, there are many other community organizations that help folks in need improve the quality of their lives and their values—food, clothing, and shelter centers that provide immediate and correctional help; food distribution programs; counseling and living facilities for abused and battered women and men; foster care opportunities; mentoring and volunteering at a public school or in a community that needs improvement, and so on.

These organizations need and deserve good mentors, volunteers, and leadership help. Some of these organizations admirably serve general needs for all youth and adults; others serve youth, adults, and families that have significant or desperate needs to improve their lives and values. Among all these great choices, find one that will provide you the opportunity to serve—one with which you feel comfortable, that matches your skills and interests, and has time requirements that you can meet and stick with. Call and make contact with your chamber of commerce; your local, county, or state government; your school district or school; your church leader; the United Way; or an involved friend or neighbor. Get on the Internet. Just get involved! And if you are already involved, could you expand your help or add one more organization or activity?

Communities need organizations that fill immediate needs for food, clothing, shelter, and financial help for those in need who qualify. That is contingent action—it provides sustaining help but does not solve the problem. They also need organizations that provide training and job support to help those in need get their lives back to self-sufficiency. That is corrective action—it gets to the root cause and fixes it. Some organizations do both. The key is to provide help for those in need to treat immediate effects and to eliminate the problem. When that happens, those same folks are often first in line to help others.

My preference is to invest my time and dollars in those organizations with programs that do both. Here is an example of one that does just that:

Melvin Bennett was a truck driver from Baltimore when alcohol and selling cocaine got him hooked, caught, jailed and cost him his job. He traveled to Florida where his life went back and forth between drugs and trying to stay clean and now has been living at City Rescue Mission, a Jacksonville helping organization, for a year and is clean from drugs. The River City Church, which works with the Mission, helped him earn money doing odd jobs, get enrolled and graduated from a commercial driving course at a community college, helped him clear up his criminal record in Maryland, and get his trucker's license back. The Mission is helping him get a local driving job and finding an apartment he can afford. He said, "I've got my livelihood back, I've got my life back." [48]

That is a program that changes lives!

Bill Clinton has written a book titled *Giving: How Each of Us Can Change the World.* In it, he details all the organizations and people he supports across the world that are helping improve quality of life and values so as to make this world a better place. He says the following:

"The modern world, for all its blessings is unequal, unstable, and unsustainable."

For all the busy, hardworking people, Clinton provides some sound advice. "Most people who want to volunteer have more limited time. For more than twenty years, the Los Angeles Conservation Corps has involved young people in community programs during school breaks, after school, and in response to natural disasters. For those who can give an hour or two per week, there are tutoring needs in every community that both adults and young people can meet." [49]

While his subject is the world, I think that conclusion also fits America in the long term. It is both sad and uplifting reading, and his stories and index provide a wide range of volunteer organizations that are working to improve America. It will stimulate your motivation and give you choices to help.

Seek organizations that can use what you can reasonably give. There are many sources.

Jacksonville Magazine publishes once a year all the local nonprofit organizations dedicated to improving self-sufficiency and quality of life. For each, it lists their Mission, volunteer opportunities, and how to get in touch. Their list includes 127 such organizations. [50]

Among all those choices, every person in Jacksonville could find one to help. Your community newspapers, websites, and magazines probably do the same. Happy hunting!

You don't have to get involved through an organization. What a thrill to be creative and do something on your own—to be a self-starter and an entrepreneur. There are three million good folks worldwide who help twenty million in need on Make a Difference Day, the fourth Saturday in October each year. Look for it in *USA Weekend*, its sponsor, or in your paper.

Chris King of Jacksonville just wanted to give.

He did not know much about the homeless so dressed as one and watched how they act and were treated. He learned how afraid good folks were as far as helping them and discovered that "Homeless people are not monsters, they are just people." On his own he collects and provides food, clothing and shoes for those who can't do for themselves through the nonprofit "Least of These My Brethren" which he founded. King just gives of himself and wants others to get involved in helping others. [51]

Edward Moore is a middle school teacher in a nonaffluent neighborhood.

He founded B.A.D.D, Brothers Accountable, Driven & Determined, a mentoring program for low-income male students. He has 45 teenage boys who meet every other week and spend many Saturdays doing community service projects at a nursing home and taking field trips to places like local colleges. There is an annual formal banquet at which the kids wear tuxes, many for the first time. "He is a very positive influence," says the assistant principal at his neighborhood school. The kids recently agreed to wear collared shirts and ties at school each Wednesday. He visits the boys' homes and they all have his phone number. Two of his "boys" who live in violent and crime-driven neighborhoods give B.A.D.D credit for helping them avoid those problems. King can be a disciplinarian when required. There are a number of his "kids" who have little contact with their fathers. One mother says, "He makes such a difference in a lot of these kids' lives. These are kids, but they are in the process of becoming men. He shows them what a man should be." [52]

Volunteers like these four that follow deserve personal praise and support. In tough times, they are the lights of Christmas.

Mark Dimond of Laguna Woods, CA, 80, rang a bell for the Salvation Army this season, raising six to eight times more than the average for his location by singing, dancing, and wearing a red hat with flashing lights.

Jack James of Christmas, FL, is going blind, but for the 40th season he personally responded to the 2,500 return addressed letters to Santa at his local post office. He included a photo of himself dressed as Santa, the words "lots of love, Santa," and paid the postage.

Tom Block of Silver Spring, MD, wanted to help the needy at Christmas but had trouble finding an agency with something for him to do. He, along with his father and friends, drove around Washington DC and handed out 33 filled stockings to homeless people on the deserted streets. That has now expanded to 15-20 relatives and friends in four cars delivering 100 big bags filled with food and clothes.

Tom Bosch, a hotel manager in Sioux Falls, SD, says an idea came to him in a dream: open the place to the homeless families on Christmas Eve. So, he opened his Holiday Inn City Center and gave 200 rooms and breakfast to the needy. [53]

This volunteer is amazing.

Billy DeLong, an eighty-seven-year-old union waiter, uses the money he earns from working 50 to 75 banquets a year to pay for his humanitarian trips to help those in need: "Uncle Billy" will travel to Vietnam to help feed street kids, and he also tended Katrina victims.

He says "My motto is service above self. No matter how old you are you can get out and help others." (54)

If he can do that at eighty-seven, think what you could do at age twenty, forty, or sixty.

When Moses Criswell was 13 his aunt moved with him to Jacksonville into a community plagued by all the things that destroy a neighborhood. But the Pentecostal Holiness Church was a sanctuary and Criswell went to college, became a minister, and preached for churches across the state. He was called back to Jacksonville to a neighborhood where "people live in constant fear" and "children are afraid to walk the streets. This is not an assignment, it's a punishment," he remembers thinking, but he and his wife decided to return. He set up a program in the church basement to "teach positive life skills" while making the church a safe haven for children on weekday afternoons. That program has been running for eight years. (55)

Joanne Hickox of Fruit Cove, FL, told officials at her church she would like to try working with seniors. That small start has grown to Barnabas International Inc., Seniors on a Mission. That includes 350 senior volunteers over 55 who gave 7800 hours in one year, to projects in 27 nonprofit organizations in northeast Florida. (56)

Use your creativity to develop one activity you could sponsor to help those who need values and life improvement help in your community.

Young people also do good things to help those in need.

Tim Tebow, Heisman Trophy winner and former quarterback at the University of Florida, wants it known and clear that, regardless of his press publicity, his achievements off the field define him more than his accomplishments on it: "Taking my platform as a football player and using it for good, using it to be an influence and change people's lives, that's more important than football to me." In March, while many of his teammates, classmates, and friends hit the road for spring break, Tim traveled to his father's orphanage in the Philippines and he visited schools to speak of his faith and helped doctors with medical procedures. He speaks and signs autographs in prisons, hospitals and youth organizations. His dedication influenced his coach, Urban Meyer, to take his family to the Dominican Republic to help feed 100 families daily and to visit a girls' orphanage. Meyer said, "Tim has done a lot of things to open my eyes . . . to have our children experience that . . . it was a life-changing experience." (57)

Thirteen-year-old Elias Farah, who plays the piano, spent 70 hours recording and promoting a CD of Christmas carols, including one he composed, to send Joseph Bond, a young burn victim, on his dream vacation to Orlando. Sales from the CD were enough to help Dreams Come True send Bond, and his family, to all four Disney Florida theme parks for a seven-day vacation. After watching several of his family members die of cancer, Elias wanted to help others feel better, at least for a while. There is always room for happiness he thought as he considered making the CD. His mother, Hanya Farah, says, looking at her son, "You always have to help in life. You already helped one person and maybe next year you can help two. It all starts with one person." (58)

Tyler Jump, a seventh grader, isn't just a volunteer—he is a superstar volunteer.

Using the Internet he has gotten people from Alaska, Hawaii, England, and France to contribute more than one million soda can tabs that are recycled and the money goes to the Ronald McDonald House charity. Periodically, Tyler, his mother, and school friends volunteer at the McDonald facility to clean rooms, wash windows, play chess with the kids, and bake cookies. He also collects toys for the charity. The article concludes, "If someone Tyler's age can do that much for the community, think of what the rest of us could accomplish—if only we had his tenacity and vision." (59)

Duane Carter did not have a very satisfactory childhood. He was homeless; he, his mom, and his sister lived in a car and then in a rodent-infested house; and he went to work at fourteen while going to school full time. But out of that came a goal:

"I strive to be something, to be successful, so I can give back to the community." He also feels, "Life's hurdles only make you stronger." He saw the value of education to meet his goal and as a high school senior he has a 3.5 grade point average and a full-ride scholarship to Georgia Tech. Carter wants to mentor others and believes there is no obstacle that can't be overcome with honesty, hard work, faith, and education. He concludes the article by saying, "If you come from an affluent background or a non-affluent background, you won't really be successful or great unless you give back and help someone." (60)

Giving of yourself to others takes a sacrifice of personal time and commitment. Among others that I volunteer and share ideas with, there is a common agreement that the benefits far outweigh the effort.

Righting the Course

Retired seniors have the time, skills, and resources to make a significant impact on improving America's values and sustainability. I live in a retirement-oriented community that is part of a small town near a large metropolitan area. Many of my friends contribute significantly of their time and resources to improve the area's quality of life and values. These folks tend to be those who have had productive and enjoyable lives, and their ethical systems include sharing and giving back from the benefits life has given them. Unfortunately, I also see those who enjoy golf, tennis, travel, and good times but give little of themselves beyond financial support. There are millions of retired across this nation. If many more were involved with giving back, that collective power to reshape America's values might just be enough to do most of the job.

If you need a little motivation as a senior to get started, I recommend an excellent book, *Finishing Well* by Bob Buford. He tells the stories of well-known people who had fabulous careers, and when retirement time came along, they didn't retire. Using their talents and experience, they started new full-time careers, mainly dedicated to helping those less fortunate climb up the ladder to a better life:

Buford says, "Success seems to make more demands than it satisfies." He quotes Harold Kushar, "I believe it is not dying the people are afraid of: we are afraid of not having lived . . . that we never figured out what life was for." Here is a way to figure that out. Buford asks, "What is your core? It is that immovable center of what you really are. It is the equipment your creator issued to you—the mental, physical, and emotional tools you've got to work with, as well as your experience and deepest passions." He paraphrases Marge Blanchard's advice to take that core, the secret sauce or leverage that was in you and drove your first working career and life, and decide how to use it toward what end to make the world a better place in your "retired" second career and life. And to close Buford adds that success, first, is using your core to satisfy your career and life expectations, and then, more significantly, to use it to serve others, that is to change lives. And from Steven Reinemuno, a top executive at PepsiCo, when asked looking back what made his life successful, "First that my kids' lives were successful and second, that I left my mark on some other men." Almost all those in the book talked of the importance of finding your core and making it the basis for your first working life and your second enjoyable life giving back. Finally he quotes Peter Drucker, perhaps America's greatest management guru, innovator, and writer of what business success is all about, who sums it all up with Ten Principles for Life II (what we call retirement):

1. "Find out who you are." What are your strengths?
2. "Reposition yourself." What is fulfillment in life's second half?
3. "Find your existential core." Why is faith critical in your values?
4. "Make your life your endgame." What can I do to make a difference?
5. "Planning doesn't work." How can I position myself to seize opportunities?
6. "You have to know your values." What values should influence my choices?
7. "You have to define what finishing well means to you." How do I want to be remembered?
8. "You have to know the difference between harvesting and planting." Where is my life now?
9. "Good intentions are not enough." What results do I want to achieve?
10. "There is a downside to no longer learning, no longer growing." How can I stay involved? [(61)]

I would not ask all the retired, including myself, to start a second full-time giving-back career. But, if you believe in the Golden Rule, I ask that you give thought to sharing your values, life, and blessings with those in need to the extent you are able.

Whether you are married, are raising children, or are a young, hardworking, single adult, take some time to think about how you could give back from your busy lives to those in need. Find or create a reasonable volunteer effort that captures your interest, utilizes your experience, and has a time commitment you can stick with. A project that involves the family or several friends would share the effort and could provide more staying power and enjoyment. Many do that, and so can you. If my premise for this book is at all correct, it may well be too late if you wait for retirement to get involved.

If you are middle aged, your life should be more stable and your responsibilities less extensive. That should give you more time to become a volunteer.

If you are a teenager or young adult, graduated or in school, what is one reasonable give-back activity you could get involved in or a project you could create? Involve your friends to increase the scope and the fun. To develop ideas, talk with those you look up to, such as friends, family, teachers, community leaders, religious leaders, school counselors, and coaches. If your parents work, an after-school project would use that often boring empty-house time.

With all of the above examples in mind and considering your stage in life, your skills and experience, and the environment and community in which you live, give thought to these questions. If you are already doing volunteer work, how could you expand that current effort? Could you find another organization or group to work with? If you are not volunteering now, what one organization, group, or individual would stimulate your interest to help? What project(s) could you create on your own? I encourage you to respond and put down your answers to these questions in the following areas as appropriate to you.

As an individual:

_____

_____

As a family:

_____

_____

As a business:

_____

_____

Now, lift your answers from the paper and into action. Hop in the boat, grab those oars, and pull America away from that vortex and back to the proud respected nation it should be. Together, we can right the course. The goal is to regain and enhance America's values so that our nation will again have the promise to provide future opportunities for self-fulfillment and quality of life for every citizen who will grab the brass ring and take it. This will take more than a village. It will take the unsurpassed strength of the vast majority of American citizens. Ambitious? Yes, but imagine the rewards. Doable? Hard, but we made it to the moon. Consequences of failure? Unfathomable, but it could be an unsustainable country for your grandchildren and those who follow. I have tried to do my part to help find a way. You have made choices on how you can help. You have a plan. Now, it is up to you. *We have the collective power to make it happen.*

The greatest reward you will ever receive is to know that someone in need has experienced an uplifting value system and quality of life you helped create.

Notes

CHAPTER 1

(1) "Prayer for our Nation," Minister Joe Wright, delivered January 23, 1996 to the Kansas House of Representatives, http://www. breakthechain.org/exclusives/joewright.html

(2) Coleman Langshaw, "It Was the Best of Times, the Worst of Times," *News Leader, Amelia Island, FL,* March 7, 2008.

(3) Jonathan Weisman, "Voter Discontent Deepens Ahead of Obama Jobs Plan," *Wall Street Journal,* September 6, 2011.

(4) Editorial, "Congress Hitting Bottom," *Florida Times-Union, Jacksonville, FL,* December 28, 2010.

(5) Editorial, "Congressional Pay, Feeling Our Pain," *Florida Times-Union, Jacksonville, FL,* January 7, 2009.

(6) Kevin Turner, "Corporate Execs: Nobody Trusts Us," *Florida Times-Union, Jacksonville, FL,* February 27, 2009.

(7) Michelle Conlin, "Foreclosure Details Troubling," *Florida Times-Union, Jacksonville, FL,* October 13, 2010.

(8) Matt Towery, "The Bigger the Con Job, the Lighter the Treatment," Viewpoint, *Florida Times-Union, Jacksonville, FL,* January 12, 2009.

(9) Opinion, "Cost Is the No. 1 Issue," *Florida Times-Union, Jacksonville, FL,* June 23, 2011.

(10) Cal Thomas, "Ingrown Waste in Washington, D. C.," *Florida Times-Union, Jacksonville, FL,* March 21, 2008.

(11) "Fraud Framework for Government," SAS Institute, Cary, NC, www.sas.com, 2010.

(12)Jonathan D. Glatner, "Colleges Profit as Banks Market Credit Cards to Students," *New York Times*, December 31, 2008.

(13) Eamon Javers, "Inside the Hidden World of Earmarks," *Business Week*, September 17, 2007, 56-9.

(14) Steve Patterson, "Anti-Fraud Campaign Has Local Ties," *Florida Times-Union, Jacksonville, FL*, December 19, 2007.

(15) Lindsey Gerdes, "MBA Students Are No. 1—at Cheating," *Business Week*, October 2, 2006, 14.

(16) Maura J. Casey, "Digging Out the Roots of Cheating in High School," Editorial, *New York Times*, October 13, 2008.

(17) Dorie Turner and Shannon McCaffrey, "Probe: Cheating in Atlanta Schools," *Florida Times-Union, Jacksonville, FL*, July 6, 2011.

(18) Michael Loeb, "Taking Home More Than Just Work," *Business Week*, July 23, 2007, 12.

(19)Justin Fox, "Self-Deal? CEOs? Nahhh," *Fortune*, November 27, 2006, 95-6.

(20) Christopher Farrel, "Do-Gooders Doing Mischief," *Business Week*, April 21, 2008, 16.

(21) "Every Child a Graduate," Editorial, *News Leader, Amelia Island, FL*, October27, 2007.

(22) Christine Armario and Dorie Turner, Associated Press, "Common Failure of Basic Military Entrance Exam is 'Shocking,'" *Florida Times-Union, Jacksonville, FL*, December 12, 2010.

(23) Michael E. Porter, "Why America Needs an Economic Strategy," *Business Week*, November 10, 2008, 39-42.

(24) Stephanie Banchero and Neil King Jr, "School Overhaul Loses Key Player," *Wall Street Journal*, October 14, 2010.

(25) Mark Schneider, "How Bad Are Our Graduation Rates," *The Journal of the American Enterprise Institute*, May 2, 2010, http://www.american.com/archives/2010/april/how-bad-are-our-graduation-rates.

(26)David Leonhardt, "Colleges Are Failing in Graduation Rates," *New York Times*, September 8, 2009, http://www.nytimes.com/2009/09/09/business/economy/09leonhardt.html.

(27) "US College Drop-Out Rate Sparks Concern," Associated Press, *US News*, updated November 15, 2005 http://www.msnbc.msn.com/id/10053859/.

(28) Frank Pomda, "Higher Education Enrollments," *USA Today*, July 23, 2008.

(29) "Employment Projections, Education Pays," Bureau of Labor Statistics, Current Population Survey, May 4, 2011, http://www.bls.gov/emp/ep_chart_001.htm.

(30) "Abortion Statistics: United States Data and Trends," Centers for Disease Control (CDC) and the Guttmacher Institute (GI), March 11, 2008.

(31) "Florida Youth Substance Abuse Level," National Institute of Alcohol Abuse and Alcoholism, *News Leader, Amelia Island, FL*, April 20, 2007.

(32) Kathleen Fackelmann, "Teen Drinking, Anger a Bad Mix," *USA Today*, December 26, 2007.

(33) Drew Edwards, "Duty of Parents Is to Protect Teens," *Florida Times-Union, Jacksonville, FL*, May 3, 2008.

(34) "Binge Drinking on College Campuses," Center for Science in the Public Interest, 2005, http://www.cspinet.org/booze/collfact1.htm

(35) Buddy T., "College Drinking, Drug Use Grows More Extreme," National Center on Addiction and Substance Abuse at Columbia University, New York, NY, updated December 24, 2007, http://alcoholism.about.com/od/college/a/casa070315.htm.

(36) Dana Treen, "More Children Use Cold Meds to Get High," *Florida Times-Union, Jacksonville, FL*, March 4, 2008.

(37) Leonard Pitts, "It Makes Sense to Legalize Drugs," *Florida Times-Union, Jacksonville, FL*, April 5, 2009, Metro, B-7.

(38) Jeannine Aquino, "Trying to Keep Teens from Lighting Up," *Minneapolis Star Tribune, Minneapolis, MN*, July 28, 2007, B 1 and 2.

(39) "Obesity in the United States," *Wikipedia*, http://en.wikipedia.org/wiki/Obesity_in_the_United_States.

(40) "Childhood Overweight and Obesity," Department of Health and Human Services: Centers for Disease Control and Prevention,

Atlanta, GA, Division of Nutrition, Physical Activity and Obesity, National Center for Chronic Disease Prevention and Health Promotion, updated February 10, 2009, http://www. cdc.gov/nccdphp/dnpa/obesity/childhood/index.htm.

(41) "Overweight and Obesity: Health Consequences," Office of the Surgeon General, US Department of Human Health and Services, http://www.surgeongeneral.gov/topics/obesity/ calltoaction/fact_consequences.html.

(42) Catherine Arnst, "America's Angry Patients," *Business Week*, November 12, 2007.

(43) "Making Kids a Priority," Editorial, Florida *Times-Union*, *Jacksonville, FL*, January 26, 2009.

(44) "Domestic Violence is a Serious, Widespread Social Problem in America: The Facts," Get the Facts Resources, The Family Violence Prevention Fund, 2008, http://endabuse.org/ resources/facts.

(45) "Domestic Violence Statistics, National," Domestic Violence Resource Center, 2008, http://www.dvrc-or.org/domestic/ violence/resources/c61/

(46) "National Child Abuse Statistics," Child Help-Prevention and Treatment of Child Abuse, National Institute on Drug Abuse 2000 Report and Child Abuse &Neglect Study, Arthur Becker Weidman, 2006 http://www.childhelp.org/resources/ learning-center/statistics.

(47) "Bullying Statistics 2010," Sources: makebeatsnotbeatdowns. org, olweus.org, http://www.bullyingstatistics.org/content/ bullyingstatistics-2010.html.

(48) Meghan Barr, Associated Press, "Bullying Has Deadly Results in Ohio High School," *Florida Times-Union, Jacksonville, FL*, October 9, 2010.

(49) Hope Yen, Associated Press, "Roles of Fathers in Children's Lives Diverging Even More," *Florida Times-Union, Jacksonville, FL*, June 16, 2011.

(50) "Marriage Statistics," US Census Bureau and National Center for Health Statistics, updated December 2009, http://www. biblenews1.com/marriage/marriags.htm.

(51) Jennifer Wolf, "Single Parent Statistics," US Census Bureau, November, 2009, http://www.singleparents.about.com/od/legalissues/p/portrait.htm.

(52) Goodwin, Mosher and Chandra, "Marriage and Cohabitation in the United States: A Statistical Portrait Based on Cycle 6 (2002)," National Survey, Family Growth, 2002.

(53) See note (49) above.

(54) "Divorce Law Needs No Tweaking," *Atlanta Journal Constitution*, *Atlanta, GA*, March 7, 2005, http://www.ajc.com/opinion/content/opinion/0305/08edudivorce.html.

(55) Roger Rollins, "'Living Together' Better Than Marriage?," *Aiken Standard, Aiken, SC*, October/19, 2008, http://www.aikenstandard.com/FeatureColumns/1019-family-and-marriage.

(56) A. Patrick Schneider II, "Cohabitation Is Bad for Men, Worse for Women, and Horrible for Children," Life Site News, *New Oxford Review, Berkeley, CA,* September 2007 issue http://www.lifesitenews.com/1dn/2007/oct/07100902.html.

(57) "Marriage, an Institution in Danger," Editorial, *Florida Times-Union, Jacksonville, FL*, December 22, 2010.

(58) David Bauerlein, "First Coast Faces Proposed Cuts, Too," *Florida Times-Union, Jacksonville FL,* September 26, 2008; Tara Kalwarski, "Extravagant Executive Pay Shows Signs of Moderation," *Business Week*, September 1, 2008.

(59) "MLB Salaries," Associated Press, CBS News, 2010, http://www.cbssports.com/mlb/salaries/avgsalaries; "Pro Football 2009 Median Salary," *USA Today*, http://content.usatoday.com/sports/football/nfl/salaries/mediansalaries.aspx?year=2009, S.F. Heron, "The Average Salary of NBA Players," Helium Sports and Recreation, 2002-2010, http://www.helium.com/items/923616-the-average-salaries-of-nba-players.

(60) Shawn Tully, "What's Wrong with Wall Street and How to Fix It," *Fortune*, April 14, 2008, 70-6.

(61) Nicole Bullock, "US Cities Face Half a Trillion Dollars of Pension Deficits," *Financial Times*, October 12, 2010, http://www.

cnbc.com/id/39626759/US; Janice Revell, "The $366 Billion Outrage," *Fortune*, May 31, 2004.

(62) "No Teacher Left Behind," Review & Outlook, *Wall Street Journal*, September 24, 2006.

(63) Bryant Rollins, "Reconciling the Races Must Be Shared by All of Us to Be Effective," Editorial, *Florida Times-Union, Jacksonville, FL*, April 27, 2008.

(64) Dave Carpenter, Associated Press, "Boomer Retirements in Jeopardy," *Florida Times-Union, Jacksonville, FL*, December 28, 2010.

(65) Katherine Kersten, "Monsters Who Beat Dad Come Straight out of Today's Culture," *Minneapolis Star Tribune, Minneapolis, MN*, July 20, 2008.

(66) "Beyond Belief," Religion, *Florida Times-Union, Jacksonville, FL*, January 26, 2003.

(67) Mona Charen, "Porn, and Its Addiction, Become More Mainstream," Viewpoint, *Florida Times-Union, Jacksonville, FL*, December 23, 2008.

(68) Devlin Barrett and Michael Howard Saul, "Weiner Now Says He Sent Photos," US News, *Wall Street Journal*, June 7, 2011; Michael A. Memoli and Tina Susman, Chicago Tribune, "Weiner Resigns Congress; No Word on Future Plan," *Florida Times-Union, Jacksonville, FL*, June 17, 2011.

(69) Toni Wilcox and Tiffany Madsen, for Project Read and Invest Early, "Dads, Uncles, Big Brothers and Grandpas Unite!" *Herald Review, Grand Rapids, MN*, March 12, 2008.

(70) Tonyaa Weathersbee, "King Criticisms Forgotten Under Dreamy Memories, Viewpoint," *Florida Times-Union, Jacksonville, FL*, March 31, 2008.

(71) Tonyaa Weathersbee, "Don't Allow Drunken Rant to Obscure Racial Justice," Viewpoint, *Florida Times-Union, Jacksonville, FL*, April 7, 2008.

(72) Rachel Zoll, Associated Press, "Pope to Visit a Divided US Church," *Florida Times-Union, Jacksonville, FL*, April 6, 2008.

(73) Jeff Brumley, "A New Survey Finds Many Are Abandoning Mainline Churches for Other Opportunities," *Florida Times-Union, Jacksonville, FL,* February 26, 2008.

(74) Dennis McCafferty, "Mother Nature Knows Best," *USA Weekend,* November 16-18, 2007.

(75) Joann Loviglio, Associated Press, "Who Pays the Toll for Shootings? You, Too," Insight, *Florida Times-Union, Jacksonville, FL,* March 9, 2008.

(76) "Studies Says 1 in 4 Girls has Sexual Disease," Times-Union and news services, *Florida Times-Union, Jacksonville, FL,* March 12, 2008.

(77) Ben Woolsey and Matt Schulz, "Credit Card Statistics, Industry Facts, Debt Statistics," CreditCards.com, December 2009, http://www.creditcards.com/credit-card-news/credit-card-industry-pfacts-personal-debt-statistics.

(78) "Incarceration Rates Worldwide," *Wikipedia, The Free Encyclopedia, Wikipedia Commons File, May 8, 2008,* http://www.en.wikipedia.org/wiki/file:incarceration_rates_worldwide.gif.

(79) "Racial Bias Persists in Drug Enforcement," Editorials, *Minneapolis Star Tribune, Minneapolis, MN,* July 14, 2008.

(80) "Hunger in America: 2011 United States Hunger and Poverty Facts," World Hunger Education Service, 2011.

(81) John Crewdson, *Chicago Tribune,* "False Claims of Military Valor 'Rampant,'" *Florida Times-Union, Jacksonville, FL,* October 26, 2008.

(82) George Carlin, "Extra Extra!," Special Edition: The AOL Reporter.

CHAPTER 2

(1) Benjamin B. Tregoe and John W. Zimmerman Sr., *Top Management Strategy,* New York: Simon & Schuster, 1980.

(2) Morris Massey, *The People Puzzle,* Reston, Virginia, Reston Publishing Company, Inc., A Prentice-Hall Company, 1979.

CHAPTER 3

(1) Brian Kilmeade, *It's How You Play the Game,* New York, NY: Harper Collins Publishers, 2007.

(2) John Rosemond, "Here's Why Parent Involvement Is Bad," *Florida Times-Union, Jacksonville, FL,* October 20, 2008.

(3) Shaunti Feldhahn, "Teens Want Control," Viewpoint, *Florida Times-Union,* Jacksonville, FL, January 9, 2008.

(4) Dennis Todd, "Teachers Not Why Kids Fail," Viewpoint, *News Leader, Amelia Island, FL,* May 14, 2003.

(5) Frederic Porcase Jr, MD, "Find Reasons to Change Behavior," Letters from Readers, *Florida Times-Union, Jacksonville, FL,* February 10, 2008.

(6) John Rosemond, "Living with Children," Methodist University, December 09, 2008, http://www.910moms.com/page/john-rosemond-living-with-6.

(7) Liz Szabo, "Report: Kid's Health Is in Danger from Heavy Media Exposure," *USA Today,* December 2, 2008.

(8) Lindsey Tanner, Associated Press, "Study Links Teen Pregnancies to Tastes for Sex-Filled TV," *Florida Times-Union, Jacksonville, FL,* November 3, 2008.

(9) Reed Karaim, "A New Era in Play," *USA Weekend,* December 14-16, 2007.

(10) David Klepper, Associated Press, "States Relaxing Penalties for Teen 'Sexting,'" *Florida Times-Union, Jacksonville, FL,* June 13, 2011.

(11) Randy A. Salas, "Modern Times Give Rise to the Bad Samaritan," *Minneapolis Star Tribune, Minneapolis, MN,* July 8, 2007.

(12) "Kid's Embrace New Technology—So Should Adults," Florida State University, *News Leader, Amelia Island, FL,* February 20, 2009.

(13) James Mehring, "Inside the Baby Blitz," Ideas Books, *Business Week,* July 2, 2007.

(14) "7 Ways to Help Your Overweight Teen," *News Leader, Amelia Island, FL,* February 2, 2009.

(15) "The Surgeon General's Call to Action to Prevent and Decrease Overweight and Obesity," Office of the Surgeon General, US Department of Health & Human Services, January 11, 2007 http://www.surgeongeneral.gov/topics/obesity/calltoaction/ fact_adolescents.htm.

(16) Mary Clare Jalonick, Associated Press, "Obesity Rates Soaring Over 2 Decades," *Florida Times-Union, Jacksonville, FL,* July 8, 2011.

(17) "Parents Often Kid's Alcohol Pushers," University of Florida; "Alcohol Most Abused Drug in Our Society," *News Leader, Amelia Island, FL,* April 20, 2007.

(18) "Live Like You Want to Live," Associated Press, Being Healthy, *Florida Times-Union, Jacksonville, FL,* May 18, 2010.

(19) Ben Warner, "Rate of Change in Technology," Community Indicators, Consumer Electronics Association, April 8, 2008, http://www.communityindicators.blogspot.com/2008/04/rate- of-change-in-technology.html.

(20) Michelle Singletary, "You Heard Me: Credit Cards Encourage Foolish Spending," *Florida Times-Union, Jacksonville, FL,* May 18, 2008.

(21) Ted Schroder, "Pastor's Corner," *Footprints,* Amelia Plantation Chapel, Amelia Island, FL, March 2006.

(22) Michelle Conlin, "Cheating—or Postmodern Learning?" News & Insights, *Business Week,* May 14, 2007.

(23) Diana Middleton and Joe Light, "Harvard Changes Course," Business Education, *Wall Street Journal,* February 3, 2011.

(24) Ted Schroder, "Pastor's Corner," *Footprints,* Amelia Plantation Chapel, Amelia Island, FL, October 2008.

(25) Khalil Gibran, *The Prophet,* New York, NY: Alfred A. Knopf-Random House, Inc., 1973.

(26) Susan Estrich, Creators Syndicate, "How Could Such a Brilliant Politician Act So Stupidly?" *Florida Times-Union, Jacksonville, FL,* March 15, 2008.

(27) "Christmas Tales 2008: Resisting Temptation," Editorial Page, *USA Today,* December 24, 2008.

[28] Justin Hathaway, "Lying Isn't the Way to a Scholarship," Associated Press, *Florida Times-Union, Jacksonville, FL*, February 7, 2008.

[29] Mary Beth Brown, "Condi Inspired by Civil Rights Heroes," Point of View, *Florida Times-Union, Jacksonville, FL*, February 27, 2008.

[30] Elizabeth Borer, "A Childhood Biography of Oprah Winfrey," About.com, http://www.oprah.about.com/od/oprahbiography/p/oprahchildhood.htm

[31] The Holy Bible, The King James Version, Acts 8:3, 9:3, 6, 19, 20.

[32] Ben Carson and Cecil B. Murphey, *Gifted Hands*, Grand Rapids, MI, Zondervan Publishing Company, 1990

[33] Al Rogers, "Amazing Grace: The Story of John Newton," reprinted from July-August 1966 issue of 'Away Here in Texas,' http://www.anointedlinks.com/amazing_grace.html.

[34] "Who Is Jesse Owens," The Jesse Owens Foundation, 1999-2000, http://www.jesse-owens.org/about1.html.

CHAPTER 4

[1] Text of President Obama's Inaugural Address, Associated Press, January 20, 2009,http://news.yahoo.com/s/ap/20090120/ap_on_go_pr_wh/inauguration_obama_text/ print.

[2] Charles J. Sykes, *50 Rules Kids Won't Learn in School*, New York, NY, St. Martin's Press, Macmillan, 2007.

[3] Neil Swidey, *The Assist*, New York, NY, Public Affairs, Perseus Book Group, 2008.

[4] Lance Martin, "Take Responsibility for Your Own Life," Viewpoint, *News Leader Amelia Island, FL,* February 11, 2008.

[5] Dennis Todd, "Fathers Key to Reducing Crime," Editorial, *News Leader, Amelia Island, FL*, October 24, 2007.

[6] Katherine Kersten, "A Father's Day Message: We Need Dads 365 Days a Year," Twin Cities + Region, *Minneapolis Star Tribune, Minneapolis, MN*, June 15, 2008.

[7] John Rosemond, "Adults to Blame for Kid's Crime Wave," Lifestyle, *Florida Times-Union, Jacksonville, FL*, January 20, 2003.

[8] William J. Bennett, *The Book of Virtues,* New York, NY, Simon & Schuster Paperbacks, 1993.

[9] Tonyaa Weathersbee, "Collective Responsibility Key to Improving Nation," Viewpoint, *Florida Times-Union, Jacksonville, FL,* January 26, 2009.

[10] Michael Hallett, "The Link Between Poverty, Violence," Point of View, *Florida Times-Union, Jacksonville, FL*, February 13, 2008.

[11] Paul Pinkman, "Court Program Helps Ex-Convicts Re-enter Society," *Florida Times-Union, Jacksonville, FL*, May 17, 2010.

[12] Paul Pinkman, "Opposition Kills a Part of Drug Court," *Florida Times-Union, Jacksonville, FL*, May 21, 2010.

[13] Shaquille O'Neal, "Join Us for America's Biggest Day of Helping Others," *USA Weekend*, October 15-17, 2010.

[14] Patricia Kime, "This Year, We're Going to Rock," *USA Weekend*, October 15-17, 2010.

[15] Geoffrey Canada, HCZ President/CEO, "The Harlem Children's Zone Project," 2009, www.soapbxx.com.

[16] "What is HCZ?: History," The Harlem Children's Zone, 2008, www.soapbxx.com.

[17] "How Our Work Is Succeeding for Poor Children and Families," The Harlem Children's Zone, 2008, www.soapbxx.com.

[18] "Sharing Information about HCZ," Practitioners Institute, The Harlem Children's Zone, 2008, www.soapbxx.com.

[19] "See Change for Kids," Editorial, Crime Prevention, *Florida Times-Union, Jacksonville, FL*, December 23, 2008; Pam Paul, "Working for Kids," Editorial, Children's Zone, *Florida Times-Union*, Jacksonville, FL, February 28, 2008; Pam Paul, "Start Small," Editorial, Children's Zone, *Florida Times-Union*, Jacksonville, FL, April 22, 2008.

[20] Tonyaa Weathersbee, "Time to Revive Black Pride Movement," Viewpoint, *Florida Times-Union*, Jacksonville, FL, March 1, 2008.

[21] Tia Mitchell, "Anti-Crime Group Gets Perspective, Tips from Youth," Metro, *Florida Times-Union, Jacksonville, FL*, February 19, 2008.

(22) Jessie-Lynne Kerr, "Beyond Social Wall to Aid Students in Academic Middle," *Florida Times-Union, Jacksonville, FL,* October 22, 2010.

(23) Tonyaa Weathersbee, "Make Education, Not Prisons, a Priority," Viewpoint, *Florida Times-Union, Jacksonville, FL,* May 10, 2008.

(24) "Progress Essential," Editorial, Dropouts, *Florida Times-Union, Jacksonville, FL,* October 31, 2008.

(25) "New York's Pillar of Strength," Rudolph Giuliani's Biography, Academy of Achievement, Washington, DC, February 1, 2005, http://www.achievement.org/autodoc/page/giu0bio-1.

(26) John Coxwell, "Let's Offer Second Chances," In My View, *Florida Times-Union, Jacksonville, FL,* January 20, 2008.

(27) Carol O'Dell, "Give Back Getaways," *Amelia Islander Magazine, Amelia Island, FL,* October 2008, 24, www.ameliaislander.com.

(28) DeWayne Wickham, "'An Amazing Story' of Giving That Could Change Our World," *USA Today,* March 20, 2007.

(29) "Education," *Kiplinger Letter,* Washington DC, January 25, 2008.

(30) Topher Sanders, "Businesses Invest in Kids' School Success Statewide," Metro, Education Collaboration, *Florida Times-Union, Jacksonville, FL,* November 11, 2008.

(31) "Labor Force," *Kiplinger Letter, Washington DC,* December 19, 2008.

(32) "Top Employers for MBAs," Career Opportunities, *Fortune,* December 11, 2008, www.fortune.com/careerops.

(33) Ken Smalheiser, "Value Driven Leadership," *Business for Social Responsibility/Fortune,* 2006, Special Advertising Feature, S2-S10.

(34) *My Starbucks: Starbucks Corporation Annual Report,* Starbucks Coffee Company, Seattle, WA, 2006.

(35) Susan Casey, "Eminence Green," *Fortune,* April 2, 2007, 61-70.

(36) Heather A. Perry, "He's Hooked on Being a Big Brother," Helping Others, *News Leader, Amelia Island, FL,* February 2, 2009.

(37) Alan Scher Zagier, "Experts Urge Alternative to a 4-year Degree," *Florida Times-Union, Jacksonville, FL,* May 14, 2010.

(38) "Who We Are—Mission," Boys & Girls Clubs of America, 2009, http://www.bgca.org/whoweare/mission.asp; "Who We Are—The Facts," Boys & Girls Clubs of America, http://www.bgca.org/whoweare/facts.asp.

(39) "One of the Top 100 Nonprofits Most Likely to Save the World," Communities in Schools, http://www.cisnet.org/about/; "How CIS Works," Communities in Schools, http://www.cisnet.org/about/how.asp; "Our network: 200 Affiliates, 27 States, 2 Million Young People," Communities in Schools, http://www.cisnet.org/about/where.asp, E-mail: cis@cisnet.org.

(40) "RSVP, Senior Corps," Corporation for National and Community Service, The Foster Grandparents Program, February 16, 2009, http://www.seniorcorps.gov/about/sc/index.asps; "Senior Corps General Background," Foster Grandparent Program, Corporation for National and Community Service, June 2006, http://www.seniorcorps.gov.

(41) "Educating Students Worldwide," Junior Achievement, Charity Navigator, 2009, http://www.ja.org/; "Evaluations: Overview," Junior Achievement, 2009, http://www.ja.org/programs/programs_eval_overview.shtml; "Programs, Junior Achievement," Junior Achievement,2009, http://www.ja.org/programs/programs.shtml; "About JA," Junior Achievement, 2009, http://www.ja.org/about/about.shtml.

(42) "About the BSA," Boy Scouts of America, 2011, http://www.scouting.org/about/factsheets/overviewofbsa.aspx.

(43) "Facts," Girl Scouts, 2010, http://www.girlscouts.org/who_we_are/facts/.

(44) "The Catholic Charities Network," Catholic Charities USA, Alexandria, VA, 2008, http://www.catholiccharitiesusa.org/NetCommunity/Page.aspx?pid=290.

(45) "Points of Light Institute," Merged Hands on Network and Points of Light Foundation, http://www.handsonnetwork.org/points-of-light-institute; "About Us," Hands on Network, http://www.handsonnetwork.org/about-us.

(46) See note (40) above.

(47) Lee Smith, "Reaching Out, Students in Free Enterprise—SIFE," *Fortune*, Special Advertising Section, S1-S12, 2007, www.sife.org.

(48) Adam Aasen, "Drug-Free, Homeless Trucker Soon to Be on the Road Again," *Florida Times-Union, Jacksonville, FL,* November 7, 2008.

(49) Bill Clinton, *Giving: How Each of Us Can Change the World,* New York, NY: Alfred A. Knopf, a Division of Random House, Inc., 2007.

(50) "Charitable Register," *Jacksonville Magazine, Jacksonville, FL,* August 2008, 69-81.

(51) Chris King, "Man Strives to Help the Least of His Brethren," *Florida Times-Union, Jacksonville, FL,* January 3, 2009.

(52) Charlie Patton, "He Creates B.A.D.D. to Do Some Good," Metro, *Florida Times-Union, Jacksonville, FL,* February 4, 2008.

(53) Rick Hampson, "In Tough Times, They Are the Lights of Christmas," Cover Story, *USA Today,* December 24-25, 2008.

(54) Joe McGavin, "He Waits on Tables and the Needy," In the News, *AARP Bulletin,* November 2008.

(55) Emily Barnes, "Moses Criswell: He Teaches Eastside Children 'Life Skills,'" *Florida Times-Union, Jacksonville, FL,* February 26, 2008.

(56) Mary Maraghy, "Seniors Spread Love with Service," *Florida Times-Union, Jacksonville, FL,* February 23, 2008.

(57) "Tebow's Faith-Based Message Reaches Broad Audience," Associated Press, ESPN.com's Automated News Wire, 2008, http://sports.espn.go.com/espn/wire?section=ncf&id=3537548.

(58) Lauren Darm, *"Teen's Music Makes a Dream Come True,"* Florida *Times-Union, Jacksonville,* FL, April 1, 2008.

(59) "A Young Superstar," *Florida Times-Union,* Jacksonville, FL, September 24, 2007.

(60) Teresa Stepzinski, "He Knew Integrity Had Value, But . . ." *Florida Times-Union, Jacksonville, FL,* May 6, 2007.

(61) Bob Buford, *Finishing Well: What People Who Really Live Do Differently,* Brentwood, TN, Integrity Publisher, Division of Integrity Media, Inc., 2004.